TRAILBLAZERS
IN SCIENCE AND TECHNOLOGY

Craig Venter

DISSECTING THE GENOME

TRAILBLAZERS
IN SCIENCE AND TECHNOLOGY

Craig Venter

DISSECTING THE GENOME

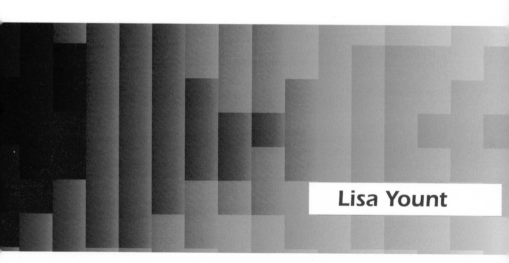

Lisa Yount

CHELSEA HOUSE
An Infobase Learning Company

CRAIG VENTER: Dissecting the Genome

Chelsea House
An imprint of Infobase Learning
132 West 31st Street
New York NY 10001

Library of Congress Cataloging-in-Publication Data

Yount, Lisa.
    Craig Venter : dissecting the genome / Lisa Yount.
        p. cm.—(Trailblazers in science and technology)
    Includes bibliographical references and index.
    ISBN 978-1-60413-662-3
    1. Venter, J. Craig—Juvenile literature. 2. Biologists—United States—Biography—Juvenile literature. 3. Human genome—Juvenile literature. I. Title.
    QH31.V385Y68 2011
    570.92—dc22
    [B]   2010050561

Chelsea House books are available at special discounts when purchased in bulk quantities for businesses, associations, institutions, or sales promotions. Please call our Special Sales Department in New York at (212) 967-8800 or (800) 322-8755.

You can find Chelsea House on the World Wide Web at http://www.infobaselearning.com

Text design by Erika K. Arroyo
Composition by Hermitage Publishing Services
Illustrations by Bobbi McCutcheon
Photo research by Suzanne M. Tibor
Cover printed by Bang Printing, Brainerd, Minn.
Book printed and bound by Bang Printing, Brainerd, Minn.
Date printed: October 2011
Printed in the United States of America

10 9 8 7 6 5 4 3 2 1

This book is printed on acid-free paper.

In memory of
Kat Macfarlane (1943–2009),
Tom Tuthill (1942–2010),
and for Vanessa,
who would have loved to go on the *Sorcerer* expeditions

Contents

Preface

Trailblazers in Science and Technology is a multivolume set of biographies for young adults that profiles 10 individuals or small groups who were trailblazers in science—in other words, those who made discoveries that greatly broadened human knowledge and sometimes changed society or saved many lives. In addition to describing those discoveries and their effects, the books explore the qualities that made these people trailblazers, the personal relationships they formed, and the way those relationships interacted with their scientific work.

What does it take to be a trailblazer, in science or any other field of human endeavor?

First, a trailblazer must have imagination: the power to envision a path where others see only expanses of jungle, desert, or swamp. Helen Taussig, Alfred Blalock, and Vivien Thomas imagined an operation that could help children whose condition everyone else thought was hopeless. Louis and Mary Leakey looked at shards of bone embedded in the rocks of an African valley and pictured in them the story of humanity's birth.

Imagination alone will not blaze a trail, however. A trailblazer must also have determination and courage, the will to keep on trudging and swinging a metaphorical machete long after others fall by the wayside. Pierre and Marie Curie stirred their witch's cauldron for day after day in a dirty shed, melting down tons of rock to extract a tiny sample of a strange new element. The women astronomers who assisted Edward Pickering patiently counted and compared white spots on thousands of photographs in order to map the universe.

Because their vision is so different from that of others, trailblazers often are not popular. They may find themselves isolated even from those who are working toward the same goals, as Rosalind Franklin did in her research on DNA. Other researchers may brand them as outsiders and therefore ignore their work, as mathematicians did at first with Edward Lorenz's writings on chaos theory because Lorenz's background was in meteorology (weather science), a quite different scientific discipline. Society may regard them as eccentric or worse, as happened to electricity pioneer Nikola Tesla and, to a lesser extent, genome analyst and entrepreneur Craig Venter. This separateness sometimes freed and sometimes hindered these individuals' creative paths.

On the other hand, the relationships that trailblazers do form often sustain them and enrich their work. In addition to supplying emotional and intellectual support, compatible partners of whatever type can build on one another's ideas to achieve insights that neither would have been likely to develop alone. Two married couples described in this set, the Curies and the Leakeys, not only helped each other in their scientific efforts but inspired some of their children to continue on their path. Other partnerships, such as the one between Larry Page and Sergey Brin, the computer scientists-turned-entrepreneurs who founded the Internet giant Google, related strictly to business, but they were just as essential to the partners' success.

Even relationships that have an unhealthy side may prove to offer unexpected benefits. Pickering hired women such as Williamina Fleming to be his astronomical "computers" because he could pay them far less than he would have had to give men for the same work. Similarly, Alfred Blalock took advantage of Vivien Thomas's limited work choices as an African American to keep Thomas at his command in the surgical laboratory. At the same time, these instances of exploitation, so typical of the society of the times, gave the "exploited" opportunities that they would not otherwise have had. Thomas would not have contributed to lifesaving surgeries if he had remained a carpenter in Nashville, even though he might have earned more money than he did by working for Blalock. Fleming surely would never have discovered her talent for astronomy if Pickering had kept her as merely his "Scottish maid."

Competitors can form almost as close a relationship as cooperative partners, and like the irritating grain of sand in an oyster's shell that eventually yields a pearl, rivalries can inspire scientific trailblazers to heights of achievement that they might not have attained if they had worked unopposed. Tesla's competition with Thomas Edison to establish a grid of electrical power around U.S. cities stimulated as well as infuriated both men. Venter's announcement that he would produce a readout of humanity's genes sooner than the massive, government-funded Human Genome Project (HGP) pushed him, as well as his rival, HGP leader Francis Collins, to greater efforts. The French virologist Luc Montagnier was spurred to refine and prove his suspicions about the virus he thought was linked to AIDS because he knew that Robert Gallo, a similar researcher in another country, was close to publishing the same conclusions.

It is our hope that the biographies in the Trailblazers in Science and Technology set will inspire young people not only to discover and nurture the trailblazer within themselves but also to trust their imagination, even when it shows them a path that others say cannot exist, yet at the same time hold it to strict standards of proof. We hope they will form supportive relationships with others who share their vision, yet will also be willing to learn from those they compete with or even dislike. Above all, we hope they will feel the curiosity about the natural world and the determination to unravel its secrets that all trailblazers of science share.

Acknowledgments

I would like to thank Frank K. Darmstadt for his help and suggestions, Suzie Tibor for her hard work in rounding up the photographs, Bobbi McCutcheon for drawing the diagrams, my cats for keeping me company (helpfully or otherwise), and, as always, my husband, Harry Henderson, for—well—everything.

Introduction

"Scientist's Plan: Map All DNA within 3 Years" read the headline on the front page of the May 10, 1998, *New York Times*. The news under the headline, Ingrid Wickelgren wrote in *The Gene Masters,* struck biomedical science "like a hand grenade."

A STARTLING CHALLENGE

The scientist featured in the *Times* story was J. Craig Venter (1946–). The article explained that Venter proposed to determine the order, or sequence, of the 6 billion small molecules that make up the *DNA, or deoxyribonucleic acid,* in the *nucleus,* or central body, of each human cell. DNA contains the instructions for carrying out cell functions that each organism inherits from its parents. The instructions are encoded in the sequence of four types of small molecules called *bases,* which link together to form the long, coiled double chains of DNA. In essence, Venter was planning to spell out what many writers have called the "book of life."

Venter's proposal to sequence the human *genome,* or complete collection of genetic material, was not shocking in itself. A large international team of scientists had been hard at work on this same task since the late 1980s in a gigantic program known as the *Human Genome Project (HGP).* Venter horrified the HGP scientists, first, because he promised to finish the sequence five years ahead of their scheduled end date, 2005. He also startled them by claiming that he and his coworkers could do the job for only about a tenth of the $3 billion that the U.S. and other governments had budgeted for the HGP. Nicholas Wade, the author of the *Times* article, wrote that if Venter delivered on his promises, he might "outstrip" the government program and "to some extent make [it] redundant."

J. Craig Venter shocked the genetics community in 1998 by claiming that his private business, Celera Genomics, could spell out a human being's complete collection of genetic information more quickly and cheaply than a huge government-sponsored project with the same goal. (*J. Craig Venter Institute*)

The worst shock of all, however, came from Venter's background. Instead of working for the government, a university, or a nonprofit institution, like the HGP scientists and most other researchers of the time, Venter headed a private, for-profit business. The HGP scientists, and many others as well, feared that if Venter's company, Celera Genomics, worked out the sequence of the human genome before the government project did, he or his backers would charge others large amounts of money to do research based on the sequence or even keep it entirely secret. "I [came] . . . to regard [Venter] as the potential destroyer of all that we had worked for" in terms of making genetic information freely available, John Sulston (1942–   ), the scientist who headed Britain's portion of the HGP, wrote in a book called *The Common Thread* (coauthored with Georgina Ferry) about his part in the genome sequencing. What the media quickly dubbed the "race" between Celera and the HGP highlighted what some people saw as the conflict between the goals of publicly supported research and those of science supported by private business—an issue that still deeply concerns scientists and observers of science today.

THE "BAD BOY" OF SCIENCE

May 1998 was not the first—or the last—time that Craig Venter challenged the scientific community, arousing both admiration and wrath. In 1991, for instance, the "bad boy of science," as a *Time* magazine article called him, had worked out a faster way to identify *genes,* or units of hereditary information carried in DNA. Within less than a year, his research team doubled the number of known human genes. When the National Institutes of Health (NIH), the government institution for which Venter then worked, attempted to take out *patents* on his gene sequences, which could have restricted their use in research, many members of the scientific community blamed Venter, even though patenting the genes had not been his idea.

Venter's later achievements, which included the first sequencing of an organism's genome, mass sequencing of genomes from the microorganisms in the world's oceans, and even attempts to create the first artificial living thing, have stirred equal controversy. In each case, Venter used new techniques that many scientists predicted would fail, but he showed that they were wrong. Each time, too, critics claimed that Venter would keep his data secret, yet he has maintained, for instance in a 2002 article in the journal *Bio-IT World,* that "there's not a single scientist who has been responsible for putting more data in the public domain than I have."

In an article published in *Discover* magazine in May 1998, James Shreeve called Craig Venter "perhaps the most productive biologist in the world." Through both encouragement and challenges, Venter has made other scientists more productive as well. *Time* magazine reporter Dick Thompson wrote of him on December 25, 2000:

> By forcing [the Human Genome Project scientists] to double and redouble the pace of their work, Venter guaranteed that the scientific rewards and potentially lifesaving medical treatments derived from decoding our genes would start to pour in almost half a decade earlier than anyone had expected.

Ultimately, Venter's rivals—and, with them, all of biomedical science—benefited from having this outspoken "bad boy" snapping at their heels.

"IMPOSSIBLE QUESTS AND GRAND OBJECTIVES"

Craig Venter: Dissecting the Genome, one volume in the Trailblazers in Science and Technology set, describes Craig Venter's life and career, a "tale of seemingly impossible quests and grand objectives," as he calls it in his autobiography, *A Life Decoded.* The book explains the advances that Venter has made in decoding and interpreting the genomes of humans and other living things. It also outlines the challenges he has presented to other scientists and to ways of thinking about the ethics of science and the use of scientific information.

Chapter 1 deals with Venter's early years as a carefree California surfer, the changes he underwent during his harrowing military service in Vietnam, and his education and first steps into medical research. Chapter 2 covers his research at the National Institutes of Health in the middle and late 1980s, including his discovery of faster ways to sequence genetic material, and the controversy generated by attempts to patent the genetic sequences he found.

Chapter 3 begins when Venter left NIH and founded his first nonprofit institute, The Institute for Genomic Research (TIGR), in 1992. It describes the first sequencing of the genome of a living organism, a bacterium, which took place at TIGR in 1995. It also presents the conflict between Venter and Human Genome Sciences, the for-profit company to which Wallace Steinberg, the venture capitalist who funded TIGR, had linked Venter's institute.

Chapters 4 and 5 detail the famous "race" between Celera Genomics and the Human Genome Project to be the first to sequence the entire genome of a human being. This competition was marred by painful conflicts, but it also spurred both sides to make astounding technological achievements. The leaders of the rival projects eventually agreed to call the race a tie, and they celebrated its ending in a ceremony at the White House on June 26, 2000.

Chapter 6 describes Craig Venter's activities in the years that followed that triumphant conclusion. After personal conflicts similar to those he had had with Human Genome Sciences, Venter left Celera in early 2002 and founded several nonprofit research organizations that he later merged into the J. Craig Venter Institute. His activities with the institute have included a world-spanning expedition to sample ocean microorganisms and attempts to create the first completely artificial living thing. Finally, the conclusion examines the improvements that the sequencing of the human and other genomes, in which Craig Venter played so large a part, has brought to science and society and the even greater benefits that it is likely to produce in the future.

James Shreeve, in *The Genome War,* writes that Venter told him in early 1999, at the height of that "war," that to him "This isn't about a race with [the HGP], and it isn't about making money, either. It's about looking for meaning in having existed." Whatever people might think of his personality and views, few would question that Craig Venter's existence has had a major impact on science.

From Surfer to Scientist

From childhood on, Craig Venter valued three things: speed, taking chances, and winning. "I discovered that I loved taking risks and facing challenges. . . . I especially loved to race . . . and still do," Venter wrote in his autobiography, *A Life Decoded*. As a boy growing up in the shadow of the San Francisco (California) airport long before the days of fences and security guards, he liked to park his bicycle near a runway and wait for a plane to take off. When the aircraft taxied down the paved strip, accelerating as it prepared to leave the ground, Craig sprang onto the bike and pedaled as fast as he could, trying to outrace the big metal bird. He always lost that contest, of course, but for a brief moment each time, he could savor being ahead of the plane.

A LIVELY BOYHOOD

John Craig Venter was born on October 14, 1946, in Salt Lake City, Utah, where his father, John Venter, was studying accounting at the University of Utah. Both John Venter and his wife, Elizabeth, had been Marines during World War II; indeed, they had met on a California military base.

The Venters and their two sons, Gary and Craig, moved to the northern California town of Millbrae when Craig was little more than a baby. The family lived in a small house in a less-than-affluent part of town at first, but after John Venter gained a better position in a local accounting firm and his

1

salary improved, they were able to move to a larger home. By this time the family included two more children, Suzanne and Keith.

Craig was an energetic boy, always skating on the edge of trouble. He wrote in his autobiography that his older brother seemed to be the ideal child, good at schoolwork and usually well behaved. Feeling that he could not compete with Gary in those areas, Craig chose the opposite role of "bad boy"—one in which he knew he could excel. When he was not racing planes (and the airport police, who eventually chased him away from the runways), he played equally dangerous games on the railroad tracks and the highway near his home.

Not all of Craig's activities were risky, however. He also loved to build things, beginning with forts and tunnels that he dug in the undeveloped land at the back of his family's property. Later, he constructed crude "soap-box" racing cars and eventually, at about age 12, a type of racing boat called a hydroplane that gave him his first taste of sailing—which proved to be a lifelong love. He liked to make objects with practical uses, such as an electronic scoreboard for his junior high school's baseball field.

One thing Craig did *not* care about, it became clear in his high school years, was schoolwork. His construction ability earned As in woodshop, and his skill in competitive swimming brought similar high marks in physical education, as well as many trophies. His grades in most other classes, however, were extremely poor. He managed to graduate from high school only because a teacher in a key class relented at the last minute and gave him a D– instead of an F.

THE SHADOW OF WAR

Craig Venter could have gone to college on a swimming scholarship, but he decided he did not want to do so. He had become attracted to the sunny beaches of southern California during visits to his maternal grandparents, who lived in San Diego, so after he graduated from high school he moved to Newport Beach, a seaside town in that area. Surfing on the beach's high waves fulfilled his love of danger, freedom, and the water, and he went out nearly every day. He took menial night jobs, such as placing price tags on toys at a Sears, Roebuck warehouse, to earn money for rent and food.

A greater danger than rogue waves soon loomed over Venter's life. The United States was engaged in the Vietnam War (1959–75), and young men who did not go to college were subject to the draft, or forced military service. Venter enrolled in Orange Coast Junior College, but he did not do so in time to obtain a student deferment, and he received a draft notice.

Venter had mixed feelings about taking part in the war. Like many young people of the day, he opposed his country's involvement in it. Still, he hated to go against his family's tradition of military service, which extended back through several generations. His father recommended that he enlist rather than waiting to be drafted, because doing so would give him more control over how he would spend his duty time. Venter could hardly help agreeing after a navy recruiter presented him with what seemed like an ideal plan: Thanks to Venter's prizewinning talent as a swimmer, the recruiter said, the young man could join the navy swim team and spend his years of service doing nothing more stressful than competing in swimming meets.

Unfortunately for Venter's hopes, the war escalated after a conflict between U.S. and North Vietnamese ships in the Gulf of Tonkin in August 1964. As a result, President Lyndon Johnson (1908–73) disbanded all military sports teams. It now seemed almost certain that Venter would have to go to Vietnam after all. However, he received a score of 142 on a military IQ test, a rating equated with "very superior intelligence," so he was allowed to choose his assignment. Venter selected the hospital corps because it was the only option that did not require extending his enlistment period. (He also had a longtime interest in medicine; he had written in his seventh-grade yearbook that he planned to become a physician.) He did not realize that this was one of the most dangerous positions in the navy.

Venter took medical training at a San Diego navy hospital and found that he enjoyed the work. He made himself so useful to the hospital's doctors that they found ways to put off the date when he would be sent overseas. After he made a rude answer to a woman officer who ordered him to cut his hair, however, he found himself not only subject to a court martial but also under orders to report to Vietnam within a few months. He asked to be assigned to the hospital in Da Nang, a large port city in northern South Vietnam, because duty there was supposed to be a little safer than service in the country's battlefields. His experience in treating infectious diseases and working in a hospital emergency room led the military bureaucrats to honor his request.

LIFE IN THE MIDST OF DEATH

Craig Venter arrived in Vietnam on August 25, 1967. As a medical corpsman, he saw horribly wounded men every day and watched many of them die. Bombs shelled the barracks where he slept, even striking his bed one day when he was on duty. After just five months of this grueling life, he became

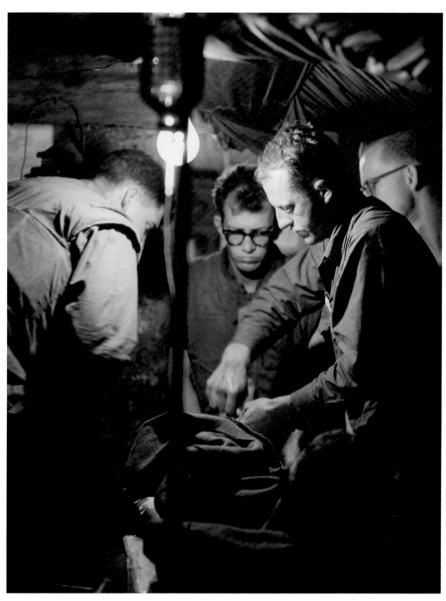

As a medical corpsman in Vietnam like the ones shown here, Craig Venter saw soldiers die every day. After Venter's military service ended in 1968, he vowed that he would make his life matter. *(Dick Swanson/Time & Life Pictures/Getty Images)*

so depressed that he decided to kill himself. He planned to swim out to sea until he became exhausted, but his own strength betrayed him: Exhaustion did not come easily.

When a shark began bumping Venter's legs, threatening to speed up the dying process in an all-too-painful manner, he had a sudden change of heart. "I wanted to live, more than I had ever done in the previous twenty-one years of my life," he wrote later. He began swimming back to shore, terrified that he would not have the energy to complete the return journey. By the time he finally reached land, he realized that he needed much more than simple survival: "I wanted my life to mean something. I wanted to make a difference."

Venter's own experience was not the only one that underlined his desire to live—and his recognition of how important that desire was. In after years, he often told the story of two soldiers who entered his hospital ward at about the same time. Both suffered from abdominal wounds, but one was much more badly injured than the other. The more severely wounded man chatted cheerfully with the corpsmen and nurses, radiating what Venter called a "magnetic life energy." The other man, by contrast, found his pain unbearable and predicted that he would not live long. He was right: He died the next day. On the other hand, the more injured man, whom Venter had not expected to survive the night, lived several more weeks. His strength and determination showed Venter "the effects of the human spirit and of sheer willpower"—a lesson he never forgot.

After his personal brush with death, Venter made greater efforts to learn medicine from the doctors around him. For instance, he became an assistant to a physician who specialized in dermatology (the treatment of skin conditions) and tropical diseases. He also cared for Vietnamese children in a local orphanage. Working with the children and sailing in the nearby China Sea became the two activities that helped him keep the horrors of the war at bay. Another new interest developed when he took a rest-and-recreation break in Sydney, Australia, and met Barbara Rae, an attractive young woman from New Zealand who shared his fondness for the water. The two agreed to keep in touch after the break was over.

FAST-TRACK EDUCATION

Craig Venter's military service finally ended on August 29, 1968. He returned briefly to his family but found himself uncomfortable with them and with civilian life. He arranged to meet Barbara in England, and they traveled through Europe together, but Venter's experiences in Vietnam had completely wiped away the carefree surfer he had once been. He now wanted to become a physician so that he could help people in developing countries.

Reaching his goal would require years of hard work, Venter knew. Because his past educational record was so poor, he would have to enroll first in a junior college and then, if he did well there, transfer to a major university for his junior and senior undergraduate years. He chose the College of San Mateo, which was near his family's home. He and Barbara wanted to stay together, but she could obtain a visa to remain in the United States only if they married, so they did so in Geneva, Switzerland, in November 1968.

Venter began his new educational path in early 1969. In addition to taking courses at the junior college, he worked in a local hospital, and he soon made himself as indispensable to the doctors there as he had done in southern California and Vietnam. His grades this time were excellent, and he gained admission to the University of California, San Diego (UCSD) in 1970. Barbara was accepted as well. Venter looked forward to continuing his education in southern California, a short drive from the ocean, which was still his favorite place to spend free time.

At UCSD, one of Venter's professors asked him whether he had ever considered going into research rather than becoming a practicing physician. When Venter said that he found the idea appealing, the professor introduced him to Nathan O. Kaplan (1917–86), a well-known biochemist. Even though Venter was still an undergraduate, Kaplan was impressed with his background, and he suggested that Venter design an independent research project in which Kaplan could direct him.

Venter decided to study a biological substance called *adrenalin,* whose effects on the body he knew all too well from personal experience. Produced by the adrenal glands, tiny pieces of tissue that sit on top of the kidneys, adrenalin governs the fight-or-flight reaction, which prepares the body to defend itself or run away when it faces stress or danger. Adrenalin is a *hormone,* a biochemical made in one part of the body that affects other parts quite distant from its site of production. It causes changes throughout the body, for instance speeding up the heartbeat and rate of breathing. Venter had felt those changes every time he took chances in a car or a sailboat, as well as virtually every day during his terrifying years in Vietnam.

FIRST RESEARCH

Some biochemicals can affect cells only after they attach themselves to receptors, protein molecules embedded in the cell membrane. (*Proteins* are a large class of biochemicals that do most of the work in cells.) Each kind of receptor is shaped to fit only one kind of biochemical, just as a lock accepts only a matching key. After a chemical binds to its receptor, the combination of the two travels through the membrane to the inside of the cell, where the chemical reacts with other substances to produce its effects. At the time Venter met Kaplan, researchers disagreed about whether adrenalin needed to attach itself to receptors in order to enter and affect cells. Together, Venter and Kaplan worked out an experiment that might answer this question.

Venter began by opening a fertilized chicken egg and removing the 12-day-old chick embryo. He then extracted the unborn chicken's tiny, beating heart. He treated the heart with a compound that separated its cells from one another and placed the cells in a glass dish with nutrient substances to form a laboratory colony, or *culture*. Each cell in the culture pulsed rhythmically, just as the whole heart had done. As the colony expanded and the multiplying cells came to touch each other, their beating synchronized. After a few days, all the members of the flat sheet of heart muscle cells in the dish were contracting at the same time.

One of adrenalin's best-known effects is speeding up the heartbeat, forcing the heart to pump blood more quickly through the body. The rapidly moving blood brings extra oxygen and nourishment to the muscles so they will be prepared for quick action. Venter showed that adding adrenalin to his heart cell cultures made the cells pulse faster and removing it made them slow down again. Working with another scientist in Kaplan's laboratory, he then developed a way to attach adrenalin molecules to glass beads the size of sand grains. The beads kept the molecules from entering cells, but the molecules were still free to bind to receptors on the cell surfaces. If adrenalin's action involved attachment to receptors, the bead-bound adrenalin should still be able to speed up the pulse rate of the heart cells. If adrenalin normally entered cells in some other way, being attached to the beads should keep it from having any effect.

Venter showed that the heart cells speeded up as soon as the bead-bound adrenalin touched them. When he pulled the beads away (using a device called a micromanipulator), the cells slowed down. To make sure that the change in heart rate was really caused by the adrenalin and not the beads, he touched the same kind of glass beads, not treated with adrenalin, to the cells. As he had expected, the beads alone had no effect.

Venter, Kaplan, and the other scientists published a paper describing this research in a prestigious scientific journal, the *Proceedings of the National Academy of Sciences,* in 1972. Having his name on such a paper was a rare

(continues on page 10)

HORMONES: LONG-DISTANCE SIGNALS

Hormones such as adrenalin send signals from one kind of cell to another, helping the different parts of the body function together. They usually travel from one part of the body to another through the blood. All multicelled organisms, including plants, make hormones.

In mammals, most hormones come from organs called glands. The adrenal glands make adrenalin, for instance. Each gland produces a different hormone or hormones; some glands, including the adrenals, make several. The inner part, or medulla, of the adrenal glands produces adrenalin and some related substances, while the cortex, or outer part, manufactures a completely different set of hormones.

Hormone molecules usually must attach themselves to *receptor* molecules before they affect cells. Each kind of hormone has its own type or types of receptor. Some receptors are located on the cell's surface, while others are inside the cell. Cells react only to hormones for which they carry receptors.

Hormones play roles in nearly all body functions, including digestion, storage and use of energy, and reproduction. Their actions are complex. A single hormone can have different effects on different kinds of cells, and the same cell can be affected by more than one hormone. A hormone can stimulate cells to make other hormones or to make more or less of the hormones they are already producing. Hormones can start or stop, or speed up or slow down, chemical reactions within cells. They can change

(opposite page) Hormones and other signaling molecules affect cells by combining with molecules called receptors. (1.) Receptor molecules are embedded in the cell membrane, with part of the molecule outside and part inside the cell. The outside of a receptor molecule has a unique shape that fits a particular signaling molecule as a lock fits the key meant to open it. A cell can be affected only by molecules for which it possesses receptors. (2.) A hormone or other signaling molecule begins its action on a cell by attaching, or binding, to the receptors on the cell's surface. Here, molecules of hormone 1 have bound to their matching receptors, but molecules of hormone 2 cannot bind because they have the wrong shape for these receptors. (3.) After binding, the combined signaling molecules and receptors move inside the cell. There, they activate enzymes and start chemical reactions that have various effects on the cell.

cell membranes in ways that let substances into the cell or block the substances' entry. They can even turn genes on or off (make them active or inactive). Hormones provide a powerful pathway through which a living thing's environment and its genetic programming can interact.

Hormones and Receptors

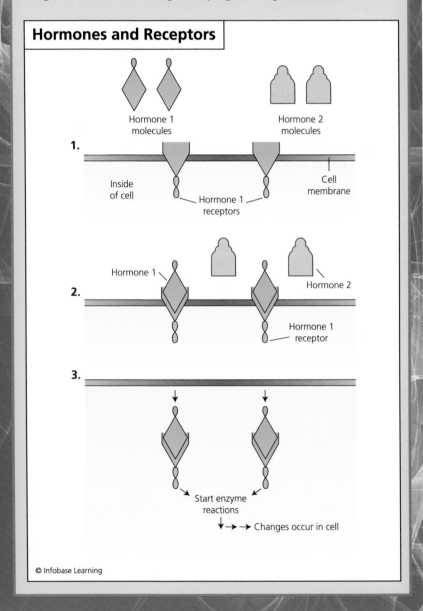

(continued from page 7)
achievement for an undergraduate. It helped Venter earn a bachelor's degree in biochemistry with honors from UCSD in June 1972.

Having decided on a career in research rather than medicine, Venter arranged (with the help of Kaplan, who now considered himself the young man's mentor) to remain at UCSD for his graduate studies. In addition to continuing his studies of adrenalin and its receptors, he used the bead technique and the chick heart cell cultures in experiments on *enzymes,* a class of proteins that speed up chemical reactions in cells or allow the reactions to happen. For instance, he studied enzymes that are released during a heart attack.

Most graduate students need five or six years to complete the work that will lead to their Ph.D. degrees, during which time they might publish one or two papers in science journals. After only three years, however, Venter had submitted or published a dozen papers, so he felt ready to move on to the project that would become his doctoral thesis. Biochemists had assumed that a drug or hormone affects all the cells in a tissue, such as heart muscle, at the same time. Because his cultured heart cells responded to adrenalin so quickly, however, Venter believed that the response occurred before the hormone would have had a chance to reach all the cells. In his thesis project, he showed that after adrenalin attached to receptors in only a small number of cells, these cells sent signals that affected the whole muscle.

Venter earned his Ph.D. in physiology (the study of body functions) and pharmacology (the study of drugs) in December 1975, a little more than seven years after his return from Vietnam. He wrote in his autobiography that he felt "proud, happy, relieved, and tired."

RAPID ADVANCE IN BUFFALO

New Ph.D.'s usually work in a laboratory as postdoctoral students for two or three years before obtaining a position on the faculty of a university. Craig Venter, however, had achieved far more than most new Ph.D.'s, so several institutions offered him faculty jobs. The one that interested him the most was at the medical school of the State University of New York (SUNY) at Buffalo, where researchers were also studying receptors. The university promised him a large laboratory and a relatively substantial salary. It even arranged a postdoctoral position for Barbara (who by then had also earned her doctorate), so Venter was happy to accept their offer.

By the time the Venters moved to New York in July 1976, Barbara had discovered that she was pregnant. Their son, Christopher Emrys Rae Venter, was born on March 8, 1977. The child's arrival thrilled Venter, but he and Barbara had come to realize that their marriage was in trouble. Craig was advancing far more rapidly than Barbara, and they no longer felt like equals. Both also soon found themselves attracted to other people. Venter fell in love with Claire M. Fraser (now Claire M. Fraser-Liggett), a young woman from New England, when she became a postdoctoral candidate in his laboratory. Barbara, for her part, moved to Texas in 1980 to join a professor she had met.

Barbara at first left Christopher with Venter, who found that he enjoyed being a single father in spite of his busy laboratory schedule. Their divorce proceedings became bitter, however, and she changed her mind and asked for custody of the child. The divorce judge granted her request, much to Venter's grief. On the other hand, his divorce left him free to marry Claire Fraser, which he did on October 10, 1981.

Troubled though his personal life might be, most of Venter's research continued to be successful. For one thing, he learned important facts about asthma, a serious lung ailment usually produced when the body's defense system, the immune system, reacts to substances to which the system has become sensitized, or allergic. Whenever a person breathes in such a substance—a certain type of flower pollen, for instance—the immune system forces the tiny airways in the lungs to constrict, making breathing difficult. Researchers had realized for some time that asthma was connected in some way with adrenalin receptors, but no one was sure exactly what the relationship was. Other scientists had learned that people with asthma have fewer of these receptors than healthy people, and Venter and Fraser found evidence that this is so because the immune system mistakenly attacks and destroys the receptors.

Venter felt that his high number of published papers and other achievements should keep his career on the fast track. Just as he had arranged to skip over the postdoctoral stage of his education, he tried in 1981 to obtain tenure, or a permanent faculty position, at a much earlier stage in his university career than it usually would have been granted. The pharmacology department, for which he had been working, refused to grant it, but the biochemistry department at the same university offered him a better position, including a larger laboratory, a raise in salary, and a promotion to the rank of associate professor. Fraser also obtained a post in the biochemistry department, and the two continued to work together.

The nearby Roswell Park Cancer Center made Venter the deputy director of its molecular immunology (study of the immune system) department, which included promotion to full professorship as well as an even larger laboratory and more money, a year later. In 1983, however, Venter received the best job offer of all: a chance to join the National Institutes of Health (NIH), the U.S. government's giant research complex in Bethesda, Maryland. He was happy to accept. As he wrote in *A Life Decoded,* "I was now ready to begin a new phase of my life."

Fishing for Genes

Being hired to do research at the National Institutes of Health was a great honor, and Craig Venter knew it. In addition, his laboratory would be well funded: NIH officials promised him a research budget of more than a million dollars a year. In short, as he later wrote in his autobiography, NIH offered him "scientific heaven."

STARTING A GENE HUNT

Craig Venter and Claire Fraser moved into the receptor biochemistry section of the National Institute of Neurological Disorders and Stroke (NINDS) in 1984. They planned to continue their study of the adrenalin receptor, a protein molecule, by determining the protein's structure and learning which *amino acids* it contains. They also hoped to identify the gene that carries the instructions for making the receptor.

All the information that a cell needs in order to make proteins and carry out the other functions of life is contained in wormlike structures called *chromosomes* that curl inside the nucleus of the cell. In most living things, the chromosomes exist in pairs, one member of which is inherited from the organism's male parent and one from the female. These chromosomes copy themselves each time a cell reproduces, so every cell in the body possesses a complete set.

(continues on page 16)

DNA: LIFE'S INSTRUCTION BOOK

James Watson and Francis Crick not only discovered the structure of DNA molecules but also showed how that structure allows the molecules to reproduce themselves, which they must do in order to pass on the information they contain each time a cell divides. Crick and other researchers went on to reveal how cells use the instructions coded into DNA to make proteins.

Each molecule of DNA is made up of two long strands of alternating smaller molecules, sugars and phosphates. (A phosphate is a compound containing the element phosphorus.) Pairs of bases, joined by hydrogen bonds, extend between the strands like the rungs of a ladder. The "ladder" twists around and around to form a long coil, or helix.

The hydrogen bonds at the center of the DNA helix are weak and break open easily. When a cell prepares to divide, it signals the bonds to release their grip, and the DNA molecule comes apart lengthwise like a zipper unzipping. Each base on the two single strands attracts its pair-mate from free-floating chemicals in the nucleus, and the hydrogen bonds re-form. The result is two identical DNA molecules where only one had existed before. Because of this duplication, each of the "daughter cells" produced when the cell splits in two receives a copy of all the DNA molecules that make up the cell's genome (collection of inherited information).

(opposite page) James Watson and Francis Crick found out that the structure of the DNA molecule allows it to encode genetic information and to reproduce itself so that the information can be passed on to both daughter cells when a cell divides. The molecule has a helix (coil or corkscrew) shape, in which two "backbones" of alternating deoxyribose (a sugar) and phosphate (a compound containing phosphorus) molecules twine around one another. Pairs of small molecules called bases, joined by hydrogen bonds, stretch between the backbones like the rungs of a twisted ladder. Genetic information is encoded in the order, or sequence, of the bases. When the DNA molecule reproduces, the hydrogen bonds break down and the molecule comes apart lengthwise like a zipper unzipping. Each of the four kinds of bases (represented by the letters A, G, C, and T) can pair with only one other kind of base. The bases in the single strands attract their pair-mates and more "backbone" molecules from free-floating molecules in the cell, reassembling two double strands identical to the original one.

When a cell needs to make a protein, it copies the sequence of the gene carrying that protein's information into a molecule of DNA's chemical cousin, *ribonucleic acid (RNA)*, creating an RNA molecule with essentially the same sequence. DNA cannot leave the cell's nucleus, but RNA can. The new RNA molecule travels from the nucleus into the *cytoplasm* (main substance of the cell), where free-floating amino acids attach themselves to the RNA in the order specified by the sequence of bases in the RNA molecule. The amino acid molecules then link together, like beads on a necklace, to form the protein.

Structure and Reproduction of DNA

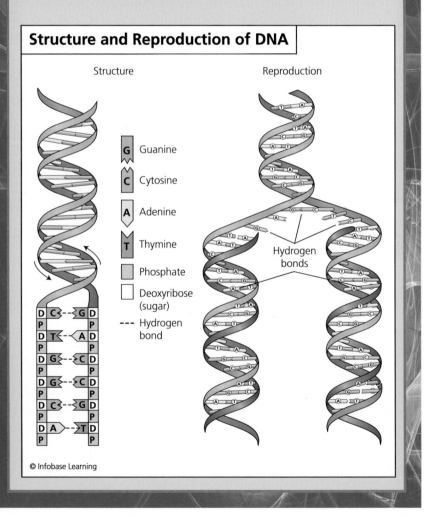

Structure

Reproduction

G	Guanine
C	Cytosine
A	Adenine
T	Thymine
	Phosphate
	Deoxyribose (sugar)
---	Hydrogen bond

Hydrogen bonds

© Infobase Learning

(continued from page 13)

The part of the chromosomes that holds the cell's inherited instruction book is a complex molecule called deoxyribonucleic acid (DNA). Just as proteins are long strings of amino acids, DNA is a long string—or rather, two intertwined strings—of smaller molecules termed bases. There are four kinds of bases: *adenine, cytosine, guanine,* and *thymine,* often abbreviated by their first letters, A, C, G, and T. A young American scientist James Watson (1928–   ) and a somewhat older British researcher Francis Crick (1916–2004) worked out the structure of the DNA molecule in 1953 and determined how the molecule reproduces. Later in the 1950s, Crick and others showed that the information needed to make proteins is encoded in the sequence of bases in the DNA molecule. Each kind of amino acid is represented by a set of three bases in a particular order. (Scientists cracked the genetic code in the early 1960s, determining which set of DNA bases stands for each amino acid.) A gene is a segment of a DNA molecule that contains the instructions for making one protein or carrying out one other action, such as activating another gene.

In their search for the adrenalin receptor protein and its gene, Venter's team of scientists first tried to separate the receptor from other substances in the cell membrane and purify it. After struggling with this task for two years, they learned that another laboratory had succeeded in both isolating the receptor and identifying its gene. Venter told the group that important discoveries still lay ahead, however. The other researchers had obtained their receptors from the red blood cells of turkeys. No one had yet isolated the receptor gene from the human brain, where its action is very important.

COMPLEMENTARY DNA

Craig Venter hoped to find the brain receptor gene by means of a tool called *complementary DNA (cDNA).* He and other scientists knew that only a tiny fraction of an organism's DNA consists of genes. Between, and even sometimes within, genes are long segments, often made up of a single short sequence of bases repeated over and over. Researchers of the time referred to these as *junk DNA,* because the segments had no known genetic function. (In more recent years, evidence has accumulated that this so-called junk in fact may carry out important work in the cell.) Complementary DNA allowed scientists to separate genes from the rest of the DNA molecule.

When a cell begins the process of making a protein, it copies the base sequence of the gene coding for that protein into a short-lived, single-stranded

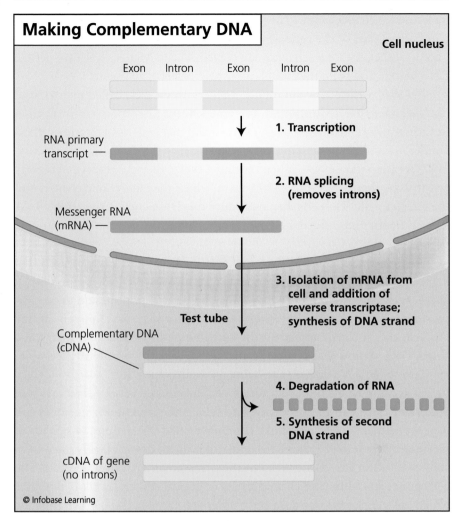

Making Complementary DNA

Cell nucleus

Exon   Intron   Exon   Intron   Exon

1. Transcription

RNA primary transcript —

2. RNA splicing (removes introns)

Messenger RNA (mRNA) —

3. Isolation of mRNA from cell and addition of reverse transcriptase; synthesis of DNA strand

Test tube

Complementary DNA (cDNA)

4. Degradation of RNA

5. Synthesis of second DNA strand

cDNA of gene (no introns)

© Infobase Learning

Genes of humans and other complex organisms often include introns, or segments of DNA that do not contain code for making proteins (sometimes called junk DNA). Working out the sequence of bases in DNA was a lengthy, tedious process in the early 1990s, and Craig Venter decided to save time by sequencing only the stretches of DNA that cells actually use. He obtained this DNA, called complementary DNA (cDNA), by a variation of a process that cells themselves employ. (1.) When a cell prepares to make a protein, it transcribes (copies) the gene carrying the code for that protein as a molecule of a related biochemical, RNA. (2.) Biochemical machinery removes the parts of the gene that are not needed from the RNA molecule and splices the molecule back together. (3.) Scientists extract this molecule, called messenger RNA, and combine it with reverse transcriptase, an enzyme that can make a strand of DNA that is complementary to the RNA strand (contains the bases that would pair with those on the RNA strand). (4.) The RNA breaks down, but the DNA is stable. (5.) Scientists build a second strand of DNA complementary to the first one, creating a stable, double strand of DNA from which the introns have been removed.

molecule called *messenger RNA*. This messenger RNA contains only the protein-coding part of the gene; if a stretch of noncoding DNA appears in the middle of the gene, that stretch is not copied. The messenger RNA carries the DNA instructions into the cytoplasm, where proteins are made.

In 1970, researchers had found that certain viruses, called retroviruses (backward viruses), contain an enzyme known as reverse transcriptase. Reverse transcriptase can make a DNA strand that matches a strand of RNA. Unlike most other organisms, retroviruses carry their genetic information in RNA rather than DNA. When they infect cells, they use reverse transcriptase to copy their RNA into a DNA form, which they insert into the DNA of the infected cells. The cells then reproduce this DNA copy of the virus's RNA every time they reproduce their own DNA, paving the way for the making of new virus particles.

Watson and Crick had discovered that the bases in the two strands that make up a DNA molecule always pair in a certain way: A always joins with T, and C pairs only with G. Because of this, the two strands are said to be *complementary* to one another. Wherever an A, for instance, appears in one DNA strand, a T will appear in the complementary strand. Similarly, the single DNA strand that reverse transcriptase makes from RNA is complementary to the RNA rather than being an exact copy of it.

Cells not infected with retroviruses do not contain reverse transcriptase, but this enzyme can be introduced into cells in the laboratory. Scientists can use reverse transcriptase to make complementary DNA copies of strands of messenger RNA. Messenger RNA molecules break down quickly once their communication job is finished, but the complementary DNA is stable. The cDNAs are stored in ring-shaped pieces of genetic material called *plasmids,* which are transferred into cultured colonies of *E. coli* bacteria. Each time the

---

(opposite page) Craig Venter and other scientists prepared so-called libraries of complementary DNA (cDNA) from different kinds of cells, such as brain cells. They used the enzyme reverse transcriptase to make cDNA copies of the messenger RNA molecules that the cells generated as the first step in making various proteins. The researchers broke the long cDNA molecules into smaller pieces with other enzymes, called restriction enzymes. They also broke open ring-shaped pieces of DNA called plasmids, which they would use as vectors, or carriers, for the cDNA. They attached the fragments of cDNA to the plasmid DNA, then "glued" the hybrid plasmid rings back together (ligation). They then inserted the plasmids into *E. coli* or other bacteria. Each bacterium reproduced several times an hour, quickly creating a colony of clones, or genetic duplicates, of itself, all of which included the plasmid that had been placed inside the original bacterium. Each of these colonies represented part of a gene that that type of cell used to make a protein. A complete library, therefore, included all of the DNA that was active in that cell type.

bacteria reproduce, which they do several times every hour, they copy the plasmids along with the rest of their genetic material and transfer them to the new cells. In a short time, therefore, each piece of cDNA has its own colony of thousands of bacteria, all the members of which are *clones,* or exact genetic duplicates, of one another.

A dish or test tube containing bacterial colonies from all the cDNAs produced in a particular cell type—which may number in the hundreds of

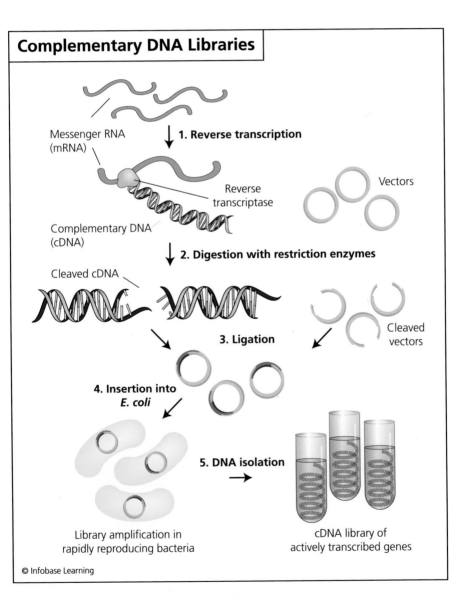

Complementary DNA Libraries

Messenger RNA (mRNA)

1. **Reverse transcription**

Reverse transcriptase

Vectors

Complementary DNA (cDNA)

2. **Digestion with restriction enzymes**

Cleaved cDNA

Cleaved vectors

3. **Ligation**

4. **Insertion into E. coli**

5. **DNA isolation**

Library amplification in rapidly reproducing bacteria

cDNA library of actively transcribed genes

© Infobase Learning

thousands—is called a cDNA *library.* Each library, at least in theory, contains complementary DNA for all the genes that are actually *expressed,* or used to make proteins, in that type of cell. (All cells in an organism contain copies of the organism's whole genome, but most genes in that genome are expressed only in certain cells. For instance, muscle cells contain genes for proteins that might be used in, say, blood cells or brain cells, but these genes are not expressed in the muscle cells because muscle cells do not need those proteins.) Scientists had made cDNA libraries for a variety of cell types, and other researchers could easily obtain them.

SEEKING A RARE GENE

One problem with cDNA libraries is that they contain many copies of some "books" but only a few copies of others. This is because cells make over and over again the proteins that their type of tissue uses most, so the cells produce messenger RNA for those proteins repeatedly. Many of the colonies in the library for that cell type therefore will contain cDNA made from this frequently manufactured stretch of messenger RNA and thus will be duplicates of one another. If a protein is made only occasionally, on the other hand, only a few, or perhaps even only one, of the many thousands of bacterial colonies in the library will carry cDNA for that protein.

To find out which bacterial colony in the library for human brain tissue might contain cDNA matching the adrenalin receptor gene, Craig Venter's laboratory team went on a series of fishing expeditions. The worm on the end of their hook was a short stretch of single-stranded DNA that they had copied from the turkey-blood receptor gene identified by the other scientists. Any single strand of DNA will attach firmly to another single strand that contains a complementary sequence of bases; for instance, a strand with the sequence G-T-T-A-C will bind to a strand with the sequence C-A-A-T-G. If a bacterial sample held the cDNA that Venter's team was seeking, therefore, that cDNA would cling to the probe segment they had made from the receptor gene.

The group attached radioactive atoms to their synthetic probe. Each time they went "fishing," they put a small sample of one of the bacterial colonies from the cDNA library on a piece of filter paper and soaked the paper in a solution containing many copies of the radioactive probe. If the paper still showed radioactivity after being washed, as revealed by its making dark spots on X-ray film, they would know that colony contained the receptor gene.

Because the gene that the group sought was not often expressed in brain tissue, they had to test more than a million cDNA colonies to find even one that contained it. Even when they finally located such a colony, around 1985, they were frustrated to realize that they had only part of the gene. To find the rest, they had to repeat the process, using the sequence they had obtained as a new "hook" and fishing in a different library. They finally isolated the whole gene in 1986.

SEQUENCING DNA

Now that Craig Venter's team had identified the adrenalin receptor gene, they wanted to determine the sequence of bases within it so they could tell how much the receptor gene in a human brain differed from the one in turkey blood. A British scientist named Frederick Sanger (1918–   ) had developed a method for sequencing, or working out the base sequence of, a short stretch of DNA in 1975. Sanger's technique was difficult and tedious, but the group knew they would have to use it because, at that time, there was no other way to accomplish this task.

To begin his process, Sanger combined numerous copies of a single-stranded version of the DNA he wanted to sequence with DNA building blocks called *nucleotides*. (Each nucleotide is a single base joined to a unit of the phosphate-sugar "backbone" that holds the bases in a DNA strand together.) He also added *DNA polymerase,* an enzyme that could combine the nucleotides into complementary chains that would attach to the test DNA.

Sanger poured this mixture into four test tubes. He then supplied each tube with an altered version of one of the four nucleotides, labeled with radioactive atoms. He put false As into one tube, false Gs into another, and so on. Because these substances were not exactly like the natural compounds, they stopped the action of the DNA polymerase whenever the enzyme happened to incorporate one of them into its growing DNA chain, much as a damaged piece of railroad track might derail a train. The chain-building process stopped at different points, so the reactions in the tubes produced double-stranded DNA segments of many different lengths.

After the enzyme had had time to work, Sanger poured his four mixtures onto separate areas at the top of a gel, a vertical sheet of jellylike material held in place by a glass plate on either side. He next turned on an electric current at the bottom of the gel. The current attracted the DNA fragments, pulling them down through microscopic cracks and channels in the gel. The shortest DNA segments, which were lightest in weight, moved the most quickly and reached the bottom first. After the current had been on for a while, this process spreads the molecules in four parallel tracks down the gel in order of size, with the lightest (shortest) chains at the bottom and the heaviest (longest) ones at the top.

Once the gel had hardened, Sanger exposed it to X-ray film for several days. The radioactive "tags" on the false nucleotides made dark spots on the film, showing where the different fragments lay. By comparing the tracks from the four reactions by eye, Sanger and his fellow scientists could work out the base sequence in their original DNA sample. For instance, they might see a dark spot on the "G" track at a position lower (closer to the bottom of the gel) than spots on any of the other three tracks. This told them that the shortest DNA segment—one containing only a single base—must be a G, and G therefore was the first letter in the sequence. If the second-shortest segment appeared as a dark spot on the A track, the second base in the sequence had to be an A, and so on.

Using this technique, Sanger had worked out the order of the 5,735 base pairs in the genome of a small virus, phi-X174, in 1977. This was a ground-breaking achievement, but Sanger's sequencing method still had many problems. The reactions could fail, the gels could crack during drying, the tracks on a gel could be unreadable—and if the process broke down at any stage, the entire procedure had to be repeated. Examining the gels by eye was exhausting, too, and often led to mistakes. Craig Venter wished that there were a faster, easier way to sequence genes.

(opposite page) British scientist Frederick Sanger invented the first method to be widely used for determining the base sequence in a strand of DNA. He began by separating the two intertwined strands of a DNA molecule, leaving only a single strand. He made many copies of the strand and divided them into four test tubes. To each tube he added radioactively labeled molecules that were similar, but not identical, to one of the four bases in DNA. He placed false adenine (A) in one tube, false guanine (G) in another, and so on. He also added the natural forms of the bases and their attached "backbone" pieces, which formed units called nucleotides, and the enzyme DNA polymerase, which could attach nucleotides to each single strand of DNA to make a complementary strand. Whenever the enzyme happened to add a false nucleotide to a DNA strand, the nucleotide blocked the enzyme, so the strand could grow no further. After the enzyme had had a chance to work, Sanger poured the four tubes onto separate parts of one end of a gel (slab of jellylike material) and turned on an electric current at the other end. The DNA strands moved down the gel, with the shorter strands traveling faster and the longer ones moving more slowly, so this process, called electrophoresis, sorted the strands by size. When the process was complete, Sanger exposed the gel to film, on which the radioactive false bases left dark spots. Technicians noted the location of the spots in the four different tracks and used this information to determine the sequence of bases in the original DNA strand.

DREAMING OF THE HUMAN GENOME

While Craig Venter and his laboratory mates were struggling to find and sequence their receptor gene, a few farsighted scientists were beginning to envision a far more ambitious task: determining the sequence of bases in the entire genome of a human being, which contains several billion base pairs. This idea was first proposed in May 1985 at a workshop hosted by Robert Sinsheimer (1920–), the chancellor of the University of California, Santa Cruz. The experts in *genetics* (the study of inherited information) who attended the meeting agreed that knowing the sequence of the human genome could be tremendously valuable. The information could help

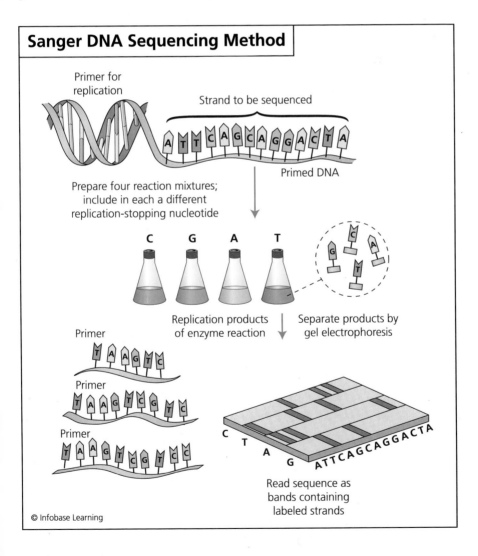

Sanger DNA Sequencing Method

Primer for replication

Strand to be sequenced

Primed DNA

Prepare four reaction mixtures; include in each a different replication-stopping nucleotide

C G A T

Primer

Replication products of enzyme reaction

Separate products by gel electrophoresis

Primer

Primer

ATTCAGCAGGACTA

Read sequence as bands containing labeled strands

© Infobase Learning

scientists identify genes that cause or increase the risk of particular diseases, for instance, or direct them to targets for new drugs. Most of the researchers felt, however, that the job would be impossible unless sequencing became much faster and less expensive than it was with the Sanger method.

Even so, discussion of the idea continued. Charles DeLisi, a mathematical biologist who directed the federal Department of Energy (DOE)'s office of health and environmental research, persuaded his superiors in 1986 to give him a small grant to launch a project for sequencing the human genome. James Watson, the codiscoverer of DNA's structure, also became convinced that (as he wrote in *DNA: The Secret of Life*) sequencing the human genome would soon become an "international scientific priority." He organized a meeting to discuss a human genome project in June 1986 at the famous genetics laboratory Cold Spring Harbor on Long Island, which he headed.

Most of the scientists at the Cold Spring Harbor meeting still doubted that such a project could succeed. Sydney Brenner (1927–   ), a renowned South African–born geneticist working in Britain, joked that the sequencing task would be so tedious that it should be assigned as a punishment to biologists convicted of crimes. Even sequencing pioneer Walter Gilbert (1932–   ), a staunch supporter of the project's basic idea, estimated that the work would require 30,000 person-years and an investment of $3 billion. Many attendees expressed fear that such a mammoth undertaking would soak up time and funding that could be better spent on research with more obvious medical benefits, such as hunting for specific genes known to be connected to diseases.

Undiscouraged by these doubts, Watson assembled a committee of top scientists in the field to make preliminary plans for the project in 1987. As DeLisi had also done, the committee concluded that the program would require 15 years, the first five of which should be spent largely in planning and developing better sequencing technology. They hoped also to work out the genome sequences of simpler organisms and map the location of known genes on humans' 46 chromosomes. Congress granted the project its first budget allotment in the same year.

AUTOMATED SEQUENCERS

While James Watson and other scientists were debating the possibility of sequencing the human genome, Craig Venter and his coworkers finally succeeded in working out the sequence of the adrenalin receptor gene in the human brain. They published a paper describing their achievement in 1987.

In addition to giving the sequence of the human receptor gene, their article compared the sequence to that of similar genes in rodents, birds, and pigs. The paper was one of the first in a new scientific field that came to be called *genomics*—the study of living things in terms of their complete collections of genetic material rather than individual genes.

Proud as he was of this accomplishment, Venter felt frustrated that finding and sequencing just one gene had required 10 years of hard and often tedious work (counting from his first studies of the adrenalin receptor under Nathan Kaplan). He was therefore thrilled to read in 1986, about the time his NIH team was completing the receptor sequencing project, that a new technology promised to make the job of sequencing much faster, easier, and cheaper.

Venter learned that Leroy Hood (1938–   ) and Michael Hunkapiller (1949–   ), then a postdoctoral student in Hood's laboratory at the California Institute of Technology (Caltech) in Pasadena, had developed the world's first semiautomated DNA sequencing machines. Instead of marking false nucleotides with radioactive atoms as Sanger had done, Hood and Hunkapiller labeled each nucleotide with a different color of fluorescent dye. This meant that all four nucleotides could be incorporated in a single reaction and detected in a single track on a gel, rather than requiring four different tracks. The gel was then put into the sequencing machine, which applied an electric current to it just as Sanger had done. As the DNA strands moved down the gel, they passed over a laser beam that activated the dyes. An electronic eye detected the colored, glowing spots and transmitted their pattern to a computer. The labels on the nucleotides, therefore, no longer needed to be identified by human eyes, nor did the data have to be entered into a computer by hand.

The idea of the automated sequencer excited Venter, who was always eager to try new technology. The sequencer existed only as a prototype, however, and Venter learned that the first few commercial models would be extremely expensive. His superiors at NIH refused to pay for one, but thanks to some scientific work he had done for the Department of Defense he had some extra income of his own to spend. He contacted Applied Biosystems, Inc. (ABI), the company that planned to make the machines, and arranged for his laboratory to be one of the sites where the new invention would be tested. What Venter (in *A Life Decoded*) called "my future in a crate" arrived in Bethesda in February 1987, accompanied by a second hulking device, a robotic workstation, that mixed the DNA and other chemicals involved in the sequencing reactions.

Venter and a technician in his laboratory, Jeannine Gocayne, devoted themselves to making the new machine work and were soon obtaining excellent data. Other testing sites found the sequencers undependable and difficult to operate, but Venter and Gocayne seemed to have a special knack for dealing with the balky devices. They found that they could analyze 24 samples of DNA at once, covering about 12,000 base pairs per day—an amount of sequencing information that would have taken a week of work to gather by the Sanger method.

Venter and Gocayne sequenced two more receptor genes in just a few months. The paper describing these genes, published in fall 1987, was the first to feature data obtained by an automatic sequencing machine. Their success persuaded NIH to pay for three more ABI sequencers, making Venter's laboratory the largest DNA sequencing facility in the world at that time.

THE HUMAN GENOME PROJECT BEGINS

Craig Venter's interest in DNA sequencing and genomics was beginning to outstrip his interest in receptors, and he felt it was time for him to put all his energy behind this new focus. Claire Fraser, furthermore, had not received the career advancement that NINDS had promised her, and around 1988, Venter saw a way to help her. The National Institute of Alcohol and Drug Abuse, another branch of NIH, wanted to establish a receptor research laboratory and offered Fraser a chance to head it, so Venter let her take over his laboratory's receptor work and transfer it to the new location. The two called this decision their "lab divorce." Not being able to work together was a painful change, but they remained close in their personal lives.

By this time, Venter was beginning to hear rumors about the proposed project to sequence the human genome. He found the idea thrilling, and he badly wanted to become involved. He attended a NIH meeting about the project in March 1988 and there met James Watson, who had long been one of his heroes. (NIH was replacing DOE as the effective controller of the genome project at about this time, though DOE remained a cosponsor.) Venter offered to teach the project scientists how to use ABI's automated sequencers, which he felt would be the key to reducing the tremendous need for time and money that had made the giant sequencing task seem so impractical. Watson, however, rejected his proposal—a decision that Watson later said (in *DNA: The Secret of Life*) that he regretted.

In the early days of DNA sequencing, technicians had to examine gels like this one by eye to determine the sequence of bases in each DNA segment. Such examination was tiring, and it was easy to make mistakes. Craig Venter hoped that scientists would find an easier and more accurate way to sequence DNA. *(Roger Tully/Stone/Getty Images)*

In 1989, Congress chose James Watson, the codiscoverer of the structure of the DNA molecule (shown here), to head the gigantic Human Genome Project. *(National Library of Medicine)*

NIH and Congress agreed in October 1988 that Watson should head the new program, now called the Human Genome Project (HGP). The project officially began in 1990 and was expected to continue for 15 years. The effort was international in scope: The United States directed it and was scheduled to carry out more than half the work, but Britain, France, Germany, and Japan also planned to play major roles.

Even though Watson had turned down Venter's offer regarding the automated sequencers, he did not reject the younger scientist's help entirely. Different scientists were choosing different parts of the genome to sequence, and Watson seemed to be impressed with Venter's proposal to sequence part of the *X chromosome.* This chromosome helps to determine gender; females inherit an X chromosome from each parent, whereas males acquire an X from their mother but a different chromosome, the Y, from their father. The X chromosome also contains many important genes, including several that can produce brain diseases if alterations, or *mutations,* occur in them. (Because Venter was working for the institute in NIH that studies brain function and diseases, he had to make sure that all his projects were related to this subject in some way.) Watson said he was sure he could obtain funding for Venter's project, but each time Venter submitted a proposal, Watson's office informed him that a longer one was needed. Venter began to feel that Watson was avoiding him, hiding behind a bureaucratic screen.

A WINNING COMBINATION

Even if his X chromosome project was funded, Craig Venter knew that he, like the other genome project scientists, would face considerable technical difficulties as the project progressed. He was still sure that automated sequencers would be helpful, but they could handle only a few hundred base pairs at a time, and most genes contain thousands of such pairs. Venter believed that, at least in theory, the best way to overcome this limitation would be a technique called *shotgun sequencing,* in which scientists shatter large pieces of DNA into fragments small enough to be sequenced, then fit them back together. Such an assembly task, however, was well beyond the ability of the computers in his laboratory—or anywhere else. The many stretches of repeating sequences known to exist in the human genome's junk DNA made the problem worse.

While flying back to the United States after attending a scientific conference in Japan in 1990, Venter had an inspiration: He would combine shotgun sequencing with complementary DNA, the tool he had used in his hunt for the adrenalin receptor gene. Complementary DNA libraries, after all, contained only genetic material known to be expressed in the type of cells from which the libraries came. These were the stretches of DNA whose sequence would be most important to determine—and they were free of the annoying repeats. By shotgunning samples from existing cDNA libraries and using automatic sequencers on the fragments, Venter believed he could find and sequence numerous genes quickly.

Venter knew that a few other researchers, notably Sydney Brenner, had suggested the same approach earlier, but most genome scientists had rejected it because they thought that cDNA libraries contained too many duplicate genes to make sequencing them worthwhile. This appeared to be the case in muscle and blood, for instance. Venter did not think it would prove to be true of cDNA from the brain, however, because that organ's complex functions require many different proteins, most of which its cells make in fairly small amounts.

Even some members of Venter's own laboratory were not sure that the new combination of techniques would work. However, Mark Adams, a postdoctoral student who had arrived just a few months before, seemed interested, so Venter gave the project to him. Adams and Venter quickly discovered that they did not need to sequence the complete cDNA in the clones they selected from their brain cell libraries. A mere 300 or 400 base pairs, the amount of DNA that an automated sequencer could handle in a single run, proved to be enough to let them check the cDNA against *GenBank*, an international open database of known genetic sequences. Anthony Kerlavage, another scientist in Venter's laboratory, called these short sequences *expressed sequence tags* (EST).

Adams's experiments proved more successful than even Venter had dared to hope. Most of the ESTs that the laboratory's sequencing machines were producing—at the rate of 20 to 60 a day—did not match any sequences in GenBank, which meant that they came from genes that were almost surely new to science. Only about 2,000 out of a predicted 100,000 human genes had been partly or completely sequenced at the time the experiments began, and Venter and Adams doubled that number in just a few months. As Venter wrote in *A Life Decoded,* he became convinced that ESTs "were going to turn biology upside down."

James Watson did not share Venter's enthusiasm. When Watson informed him in April 1991 that one of his chromosome-sequencing proposals had finally been accepted, Venter asked that the money earmarked for that project be given to his new EST work instead. Watson refused—and Venter startled everyone by turning down the grant. The old ways of sequencing no longer interested him.

PATENTING GENES

Shortly after Craig Venter had rejected James Watson's funding offer, Venter happened to lose his way in the maze of buildings on the NIH campus and asked a passerby for directions. The man he stopped proved to be Reid Adler, the head of NIH's technology transfer office. (Technology transfer is the process of moving scientific discoveries from universities or government-sponsored institutions like NIH to the business arena, where private companies can develop commercial products from them.) Adler told Venter that in fact he had been looking for him; he wanted to talk to him about patents.

When an inventor obtains a patent on an invention or process, the government gives him or her the exclusive right to sell or profit from the invention for a certain period of time. In return, the inventor must publish the details of the invention so that others can use it after the time period has expired. In 1980, the U.S. Supreme Court ruled that even living things could be patented, if an inventor had altered them significantly from their natural form. Courts soon extended patenting privileges to genes and parts of genes as well.

Such patents had become very important in the biotechnology industry, which depends largely on bacteria and other living things whose genes have been modified by humans. *Biotechnology*—the use of other organisms, especially microorganisms, to benefit humankind—has existed throughout human history, but its modern form originated in the early 1970s when two scientists in California invented a technique for transferring genetic material from one organism, or even one species, to another and making it active in its new location. Thus, for instance, researchers could transplant a human gene into a bacterium and thereby make the bacterium able to produce the protein for which that gene carried the code, even if it could not have done so in its natural state. Each time the bacterium reproduced, furthermore, it passed the new gene on to both of its daughter cells along with its own genome. Colonies of bacteria created with this technique, which came to be called *genetic engineering,* could become factories for making human proteins used as drugs. By the time Reid Adler met Craig Venter, medicines produced by genetically altered, patented bacteria had made a great deal of money for a few biotechnology companies.

Adler told Venter that representatives of a biotechnology business had heard about his laboratory's work and asked whether NIH was planning to take out patents on the ESTs that Venter and Adams were discovering. The company recommended doing so because the ESTs might be valuable to companies trying to develop drugs against diseases involving the genes to which the ESTs belonged. Adler agreed, he said—and so, in effect, did the government. In 1980, Congress had passed the Bayh-Dole Act, which permitted, and indeed encouraged, universities and research institutions to patent discoveries and inventions that their scientists created. The institutions could then make arrangements with for-profit businesses to develop and sell those inventions. The act applied even to institutions funded by the government itself, such as NIH.

Venter rejected the idea of patenting his ESTs at first. Like many other scientists, he believed that patenting genes or parts of genes potentially hindered research by allowing individuals or companies to "own" the genes they discovered. They then could either keep information about the genes secret or charge other scientists high prices for permission to work with them.

Adler insisted that just the opposite was the case. Once a patent was obtained, he pointed out, the details of the patented invention *had* to be published—just the opposite of the secrecy that Venter feared. Patents also do not apply to academic research, so scientists in universities or institutes like NIH would not have to pay to experiment with patented genes. In fact, Adler claimed, patenting helps both science and society because it encourages transformation of scientists' discoveries into practical products. The holder of a gene patent could promise a company the exclusive right to sell and profit from products made from that gene, which would give the company a chance to earn back money it spent on developing the products. Without such a promise, pharmaceutical or biotechnology firms would be unlikely to make the considerable investment needed to develop new drugs or medical tests.

NIH also had another reason for wanting to submit patent applications on Venter's ESTs, Adler went on. Although patents on genes and even parts of genes had been granted, the law was not clear about whether something like an EST could be patented—and NIH wanted to find out. In order for an invention to be patentable, it must be new, nonobvious, and useful. Venter's ESTs clearly met the first two of these three standards, but the third potentially presented an obstacle. No one yet knew which genes the ESTs came from, let alone what the genes' normal functions were or what products, if any, might be developed from them. About the only useful purpose that could be claimed for an EST was that it could be used as a probe, or "fishing hook," to help researchers locate its gene in a longer stretch of DNA. No one was sure whether patent officers would consider this to be sufficient to meet the usefulness test. Their decision on the EST patents could reveal their thinking.

EXPLOSIVE REACTIONS

After some discussion, Venter agreed to cooperate with Adler's efforts. A major paper about Venter's first group of ESTs—337 of them—was already scheduled to appear in the prestigious journal *Science* in about a month, however, and Venter insisted that this publication not be delayed. The application for a patent on the ESTs therefore would have to be filed quickly, because such an application must be submitted before a description of the invention is published. Adler filed the application on June 20, 1991, the day before the Venter team's paper, "Complementary DNA Sequencing: Expressed Sequence Tags and Human Genome Project," appeared in print.

Few scientists knew about the NIH patent application at that time, but the EST paper in itself drew both praise and controversy. The paper's authors stated that using cDNA and ESTs could let researchers identify most human genes without carrying out the complete sequencing that the Human Genome Project was planning, potentially making a great reduction in the time and cost of the project without losing its benefits to science and medicine. *Science*'s editor, Daniel E. Koshland, Jr. (1920–2007), agreed, writing in an editorial that the Venter laboratory had found "a shortcut of immediate practicality and great interest to the understanding of the human genome. . . . Lighthouses are being provided along the chromosomes to guide the way for weary sequencers."

Some other scientists whom Leslie Roberts quoted in a news article in the same issue, however, were less optimistic. In the paper, Venter and his team admitted that their technique could not find all human genes, but they predicted that it could locate 80 to 90 percent of them. British molecular biologist John Sulston told Roberts, "I think 8 or 9 percent [would be] more like it." Watson and the other HGP scientists also said they felt that Venter's approach would miss crucial genetic information contained in promoters, DNA sequences outside the genes (and therefore not copied into messenger RNA) that determine when and where genes are activated.

The patent question moved to center stage in discussions of Venter's work after Venter mentioned NIH's patent application during a hearing on the Human Genome Project before a Senate committee in July. James Watson, who also attended the hearing, exploded, claiming that applying for patents on such small parts of genes was "sheer lunacy" and that the idea "horrified" him. He also belittled Venter's EST technique, saying that "virtually any monkey" could perform it. Watson (and, later, other critics as well) complained that patenting ESTs might deny patents to later scientists who did more important work on the same genes, such as determining the genes' function, and would discourage industry from developing products based on the genes because they might not be able to obtain patent protection for the products. This was the exact opposite of Adler's, and by now Venter's, argument in favor of patenting the sequences.

Venter wrote in *A Life Decoded* that Watson's reaction startled as well as dismayed him because Watson "had known about the patents for months" and had had many chances to state his objections privately. Instead, Watson chose to criticize the patent application in this very public way and, furthermore, to suggest—incorrectly—that the application had been Venter's idea. Venter agreed with Christopher Anderson, a reporter for the European science journal *Nature*, that the real reason Venter's work disturbed Watson and other supporters of the Human Genome Project was a fear that his streamlined technique would make Congress conclude that spending the time and money to sequence the complete human genome was unnecessary.

Some news stories about the arguments at the hearing expressed the fear that the NIH patent application would set off a genomic "gold rush," in which competing scientists, institutions, and even countries might race to lay claim to pieces of the human genetic code. Several genetics societies protested against the NIH patents for this reason. They also claimed that patenting could slow or block the free exchange of information that is so important to science. In vain, Venter and others who supported the patenting process pointed out that applying for a patent on a DNA sequence did not hide the sequence from the scientific community. Venter could place his EST sequences in GenBank or any other database after a patent application was filed.

The patent controversy became worse in early 1992, when NIH applied for a patent on 2,375 more ESTs from the human brain that Venter's group had discovered by then. This dispute over gene patenting, among other things, caused growing tension between James Watson and Bernadine Healy (1944–   ), then head of NIH. Their disagreements finally led Watson to resign as director of the Human Genome Project on April 10, 1992.

A NEW INSTITUTE

Craig Venter found the argument over patenting to be merely an irritating distraction. He did not care whether money could be made from these discoveries; the discoveries themselves, and above all, the improved techniques that had made them possible, were his only concern. He insisted that the techniques remain in the public domain, so any scientist could use them without having to obtain a license from NIH or the U.S. government.

Venter might not have been seeking profit from his new gene collection, but others were. Several times in early 1992, biotechnology companies and venture capitalists (people who invest money in new companies) tried to persuade him to leave NIH and either join an existing business or start a new company centering on his work. At first, he told them he was not interested. Money, even large amounts of it, was not enough for him: He wanted his own institute—and he wanted it to be nonprofit.

One venture capitalist was willing to meet Venter's terms, but he had some requirements of his own. Wallace Steinberg (1934–95), owner of HealthCare Ventures, told Venter that he could have his institute, but it would have to be linked to a new for-profit company, Human Genome Sciences (HGS), that Steinberg would also own. HGS would have the exclusive right, for a limited time, to develop commercially any discoveries that Venter or other scientists at his institute made. Venter accepted Steinberg's offer on June 10, 1992, although he worried (he wrote in his autobiography) that he was "signing a deal with the devil."

The new institute, Venter and Steinberg agreed, would be called The Institute for Genomic Research. Venter insisted that the T in *the* be capitalized, so that the abbreviation for the institute would be TIGR—pronounced *tiger*. Craig Venter planned to make sure that before long, all of bioscience would hear his "tiger" roar.

Spelling Out the Code

Craig Venter was thrilled to have what most scientists could only dream of: his own institute, almost unlimited funding for it—Steinberg promised him $10 million to start and another $60 million to be spread over the following 10 years—and a substantial sum in his own pocket. From the beginning, however, he was uneasy about The Institute for Genomic Research's sister company, Human Genome Sciences (HGS). He was happy to have the institute's discoveries become the basis for commercial products, because that would potentially make them useful to doctors and patients. He was concerned, however, about the limits Steinberg placed on his release of data to other scientists. Steinberg required that HGS have the right to review all data from TIGR for six months to determine whether it might have commercial potential and file patent applications on it if the company wished, before it could be published. If HGS judged certain genetic sequences likely to be especially valuable, it could keep exclusive rights to them for as much as an additional year.

In fact, writers such as James Shreeve have pointed out, many for-profit companies imposed similar requirements on scientists who had contracts with them. Venter had already felt his fellow scientists' wrath because of his involvement in NIH's patenting attempts, however, and he feared that HGS's withholding of data might darken their views of him even more.

Worries about data sharing were not the only reason for Venter's unease. According to Ingrid Wickelgren's book *The Gene Masters,* Venter disliked William Haseltine (1944–   ), the man who Steinberg chose to head HGS, from the moment the two met in July 1992—and the feeling was mutual. Haseltine had a scientific background: He had done significant work on AIDS, and, until he took over HGS, he was a professor at Harvard University. Nonetheless, he and Venter had very different plans for TIGR and HGS. Venter saw HGS's main purpose as issuing licenses to commercialize discoveries made at TIGR, but Haseltine planned to have HGS itself develop drugs based on TIGR's genetic information. James Shreeve writes that Haseltine saw Venter merely as an expendable "booster rocket" that could give HGS a head start on collecting such information. Haseltine planned to set up a competing facility for gene sequencing that ultimately would be far larger than TIGR's. Once he achieved that goal, he would dispense with Venter and TIGR.

Putting his fears aside for the time being, Venter concentrated on setting up his new institute. TIGR's home was a former ceramics factory in Rockville,

Craig Venter called his new nonprofit institute The Institute for Genomic Research. He insisted that the first letter of *the* be capitalized so that the institution's initials would spell TIGR (pronounced *tiger*). This photograph shows TIGR's headquarters in Rockville, Maryland, in 1997. *(Jean-Christian Bourcart/Liaison Agency/Getty Images)*

Maryland, a few miles north of Bethesda. In addition to Venter himself, its staff included Fraser, Mark Adams, and seven other scientists who had left NIH with them. Venter installed six automated sequencing machines that he already owned, then ordered 20 more; altogether, they would let TIGR sequence about 100 million base pairs of DNA a year. Both TIGR and HGS became operational in January 1993.

TIGR's first project, Venter decided, would be sequencing ESTs from the expressed DNA in every major organ and tissue in the human body and assembling them into a huge database. Venter called this the Human Gene Anatomy Project. Libraries of complementary DNA had never been made for most organs and tissues, so the group had to create them. To do so, they obtained tissue samples from a wide variety of sources, representing people of different ages, races, and states of health.

NEW FRIEND, NEW PROJECT

Craig Venter made a valuable new friend in early 1993, soon after TIGR opened. At a genetics conference in Bilbao, Spain, he met Hamilton Smith (1931–   ), a biochemist from Johns Hopkins University. Although Smith seldom mentioned the fact, he had won a Nobel Prize in physiology or medicine in 1978. He earned the award for his discovery in the late 1960s of restriction enzymes, substances that bacteria use to defend themselves against viruses by breaking up the viruses' DNA. Genetic engineers relied on these "molecular scissors" to cut genes out of one genome and paste them into another.

Venter wrote in *A Life Decoded* that when he introduced himself, Smith said, "I thought you were supposed to have horns," referring to the demonic reputation that Venter had come to have among some scientists. Smith, a quiet man, was the personal opposite of the outgoing Venter, but the two men liked each other at once. "My guess is, we both wish we could be a little more like the other person," Venter later told Kevin Davies, who quoted him in a book called *Cracking the Genome*.

At the end of the conference, Venter invited Smith to join TIGR's scientific advisory board, a group that met twice a year to evaluate the institute's projects. Smith accepted, and he attended his first board meeting in September 1993. The human EST library program was winding down by this time, and Venter was looking for a new research project. Smith proposed one: sequencing the genome of *Hemophilus influenzae,* the bacterium in which he had discovered his first restriction enzyme. Despite its name, this bacterium

Nobel Prize–winner Hamilton Smith, shown here, helped Craig Venter sequence many kinds of genomes, beginning with bacteria. The two men also became lifelong friends. In the late 2000s, Smith led a project that was attempting to synthesize a living microorganism from inert chemicals. *(J. Craig Venter Institute)*

does not cause influenza. Instead, it produces serious ear, lung, and brain infections in children.

Sequencing the entire genome of even a mere bacterium would be no mean task, Smith and Venter knew. Researchers had spelled out the genomes of a few viruses, but the genomes of even the smallest living things—bacteria and other single-celled microorganisms—are many times larger than those of viruses. (Viruses are not considered to be living things because they cannot reproduce on their own.) The *Hemophilus* genome, for instance, was thought to contain about 1.8 million base pairs, as opposed to only about 50,000 base pairs for viruses. If the TIGR group could become the first to sequence the complete genome of a living organism, they would achieve a major scientific milestone.

Smith admitted that the project was risky. It would take over all of TIGR's resources for some time. If it failed, the company's reputation and even perhaps its survival could be threatened. Those very features, however, apparently appealed to the risk taker in Craig Venter. According to Ingrid Wickelgren's *The Gene Masters,* Venter became enthusiastic about Smith's idea immediately, crying "Let's do it!"

A POSSIBLE SHORTCUT

Most scientists working on sequencing projects, including those taking part in the Human Genome Project, proceeded in three steps. First, they broke the genome or other large stretch of DNA into small parts, each of which they cloned many times by inserting it into bacteria. They then arranged the parts in order by sequencing the ends of each of the scraps and looking for sequences that overlapped, creating a map of contiguous segments, or *contigs*. Finally, they sequenced the full length of each segment. Smith originally planned to follow this process with *Hemophilus influenzae*, carrying out the cloning and mapping stages in his own laboratory at Johns Hopkins. The other scientists in the laboratory, however, complained that the work would be tedious, and they had no grant money to pay for it.

Smith then had an inspiration. Perhaps, he thought, the researchers could save time by eliminating the mapping stage, instead shattering the genome into millions of tiny pieces all at once and then sequencing the individual pieces. After the sequencing was done, they would feed the sequences into a computer and let the computer compare the sequences to determine their order in the original genome. This procedure, called *whole-genome shotgun sequencing*, had worked with virus genomes, but no one had tried it with anything as large as the genome of a bacterium.

Smith was not sure that the computers of the time could put together such a complex jigsaw puzzle. However, TIGR's chief computer expert, Granger Sutton, had written a program called the TIGR Assembler, which ran on several powerful computers at the same time (parallel computing). By comparing the sequences of thousands of ESTs to one another, the program had successfully linked a number of the fragments together to spell out whole genes. Smith hoped it could handle the task of reassembling his bacterial Humpty Dumpty as well.

MAJOR CHANGES

As Craig Venter and Hamilton Smith planned their new project, their rivals at Human Genome Sciences were also hard at work. Haseltine and Steinberg had pulled off a coup for that company in May 1993 by signing a contract with SmithKline Beecham (now GlaxoSmithKline), a large British pharmaceutical firm. George Poste, SmithKline Beecham's farsighted research director, realized that information about the genes of humans and other organisms, such as bacteria, could help drug designers target processes in

FRANCIS COLLINS: LEADER OF THE HUMAN GENOME PROJECT

By the time Bernadine Healy appointed Francis Sellers Collins to head the Human Genome Project in 1993, he had already discovered the genes that cause several inherited diseases. He was born in Staunton, Virginia, on April 14, 1950, and grew up on a farm near there. His parents were drama teachers who had left New York City for rural life. Collins was the youngest of their four sons.

Collins began in physical science, earning a B.S. in chemistry from the University of Virginia in 1970 and a Ph.D. in physical chemistry from Yale University in 1974. During his graduate studies, however, he took a biochemistry course that turned his interest to life science. After completing his Ph.D., he enrolled in medical school at the University of North Carolina, Chapel Hill, from which he earned his M.D. with honors in 1977. While in medical school, he became fascinated by human genetics.

Francis Collins, shown here, took over the directorship of the Human Genome Project in 1993, after James Watson resigned. Collins later became head of the National Institutes of Health. He has also identified the genes that cause several inherited diseases. (*National Institutes of Health*)

Collins became an assistant professor of internal medicine and human genetics at the University of Michigan in 1984. He decided to specialize in seeking genes that, in mutated form, are responsible for inherited diseases. As Craig Venter also learned, finding a particular gene at this time was a tedious task that could require years of work. In the early

(*continues*)

(continued)

1980s, while a postdoctoral fellow at Yale, Collins had developed a technique that speeded up the process considerably. In effect, it allowed gene hunters to leapfrog over large stretches of DNA rather than painstakingly "walking" from base to base as they had had to do before.

Using this method and others he had invented, Collins collaborated with a Taiwan-born Canadian researcher Lap-Chee Tsui (1950–   ) to locate the gene that causes cystic fibrosis in 1989. Cystic fibrosis makes thick, sticky mucus accumulate in the lungs, leading to constant lung infections and, often, an early death. Collins and Tsui's discovery marked the first time that scientists had found a gene without having any idea where it lay among the chromosomes. Collins went on to discover the genes behind several other inherited illnesses.

As director of NIH's National Human Genome Research Institute (NHGRI), Collins oversaw the Human Genome Project and related research from 1993 to 2008. He was involved not only in "racing" Craig Venter to work out the initial sequence of the human genome, but in "finishing" the sequence—closing the gaps in the initial, rough draft version. This final phase of the project concluded in April 2003, the 50th anniversary of Watson and Crick's discovery of the structure of DNA. Collins and other HGP scientists also sequenced the genomes of the mouse and other organisms, analyzed the human genome, and prepared a catalog of human genetic variations. Collins continued his research on individual disease-related genes as well, discovering genes connected with the most common form of diabetes (adult-onset, or type 2, diabetes).

Collins resigned from NHGRI in May 2008. President Barack Obama (1961–   ) chose him to head the entire National Institutes of Health, and he assumed that position on August 17, 2009. Obama also awarded Collins the National Medal of Science, the highest civilian award that the U.S. government can give to a scientist, in October 2009.

sick and healthy cells more accurately than had ever been possible before. At Poste's urging, SmithKline Beecham agreed to pay $125 million to HGS for the exclusive right to create drugs from Venter's genetic discoveries. Haseltine used some of the pharmaceutical company's money to set up sequencing facilities at HGS. By the end of 1993, HGS had almost five times more sequencing capacity than TIGR.

NIH and the Human Genome Project were also going through major changes. Bernadine Healy appointed Francis Collins (1950–   ) to replace James Watson as director of the HGP, and Collins took over the project at the beginning of 1993. Later that year, after a change in political administration, Healy herself resigned.

Unlike Healy, her successor, Harold Varmus (1939–   ), did not approve of patenting genetic sequences whose function was not known. He therefore did not appeal the patent office's decision to reject NIH's applications for patents on Venter's ESTs. The question of whether ESTs were patentable therefore remained answered, and it is still not entirely settled today. On the whole, however, courts have held that ESTs representing genes of unknown function are not useful enough to be patented.

INSTANT GENE SEARCH

TIGR's database of human genes proved its worth spectacularly in late 1993, when it helped a Johns Hopkins University scientist named Bert Vogelstein (1949–   ) identify genes that play an important part in hereditary nonpolyposis colon (large intestine) cancer, thought to be the most common inherited disease in humans. Vogelstein suspected that these genes would prove to be similar to genes in microorganisms that repair errors in DNA reproduction. A mutation in such a gene could leave errors uncorrected, and if those errors occurred in genes governing growth, cells containing them might become cancerous.

Sifting through cDNA libraries to hunt for human genes with sequences similar to those of the microbial genes would have taken months, perhaps years. Instead, Vogelstein and his research partner, Kenneth Kinzler, telephoned Venter and asked him whether he knew of any human ESTs that looked similar to bacterial DNA repair genes. Venter used computer software to search the TIGR database and found three such genes within minutes. Vogelstein went on to show that one of these genes was mutated in about 30 percent of patients with this form of colon cancer, and the other genes also affected people's risk of developing colon cancer. Other researchers were impressed when Vogelstein published his work in 1994 and explained how he had found the genes.

Vogelstein's find was not the only good news that Venter received at this time. Human Genome Sciences put its stock on public sale for the first time at the end of 1993, and the share price rose rapidly. Wallace Steinberg had given Venter 10 percent of HGS's stock when the company was formed, and *New York Times* science reporter Nicholas Wade estimated in February 1994 that those shares were then worth no less than $12 million.

Venter's stock windfall existed only on paper, however, whereas his frustration with HGS and William Haseltine was all too real. HGS allowed academic researchers to access TIGR's database of ESTs through the company's Web site, but Haseltine insisted that anyone using the database allow HGS to review scientific papers growing out of the TIGR data before the papers were published. Database users also had to give the company first option on selling any commercial products based on the data. Most scientists refused to accept these terms, and many again criticized Venter for controlling genetic information for profit, even though Venter in fact tried repeatedly to persuade the HGS board of directors to change the company's policy. The strain of this conflict grew so severe that it affected Venter's health. He developed diverticulitis, a form of colon inflammation associated with stress, and had to have part of his intestine removed in 1994.

SEQUENCING A BACTERIAL GENOME

Craig Venter's painful relationship with William Haseltine and Human Genome Sciences made him all the more eager to begin his new project of sequencing the *Hemophilus influenzae* genome. TIGR applied to NIH for a grant to pay for this work in mid-1994, but Venter knew that NIH was skeptical of whole-genome shotgun sequencing and thus was unlikely to provide the funding. He therefore used some of TIGR's own money to launch the project instead.

Hamilton Smith, still at Johns Hopkins, began the work by mechanically shredding numerous copies of *Hemophilus* DNA (from a strain of the bacterium rendered unable to cause disease) into more than a million pieces, about 100,000 of which he inserted into plasmids that he then transferred into bacteria. He let the bacteria multiply into separate colonies of clones, creating a library of duplicated fragments much like the cDNA libraries that Venter had used earlier. The library was ready for TIGR in February 1994.

After sequencing several hundred sample clones as a test, the TIGR group began its main sequencing task in April. By late summer, they had worked out the code letters in around 25,000 randomly selected pieces of DNA, each about 500 base pairs long. They fed these sequences into the TIGR Assembler program, which connected them into long contigs. The sci-

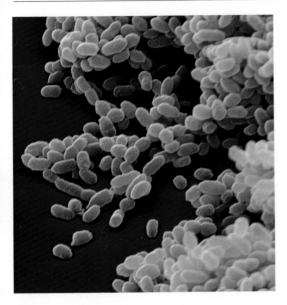

The first living thing to have its genome sequenced was the bacterium *Hemophilus influenzae,* shown here. This bacterium does not cause flu, but it can produce serious ear, lung, and brain diseases in children. *(Eye of Science/Photo Researchers, Inc.)*

entists then filled in the gaps between the contigs by examining the sequences at each end of the long segments and pairing them with complementary sequences at the ends of other contigs. Venter had to laugh when NIH, as expected, rejected TIGR's grant application in September; his team had almost completed the task that the government institutes claimed was impossible!

The TIGR team finished sequencing the *Hemophilus influenzae* genome in April 1995. They also analyzed many of the microbe's approximately 1,700 genes. They began the analysis by searching through GenBank and other databases for similar genetic sequences in other organisms, because the chances were good that if a gene was known to make a certain protein in, say, another bacterium, a gene with about the same base sequence in *H. influenzae* would prove to make a similar protein. They assembled the genes whose functions they could guess into a chart showing the functions and the relationships between the genes. They found more than 40 percent of *H. influenzae*'s genes did not match any other genes whose functions were known.

While most of the TIGR scientists were working on *H. influenzae,* Claire Fraser headed a small group that sequenced the genome of a tiny parasitic bacterium called *Mycoplasma genitalium.* This tiny bacterium, which lives in the human genital tract, interested Venter because it had the smallest genome of any living organism known at the time. Venter wondered if a simplified version of that genome might be used as the basis for a truly daring

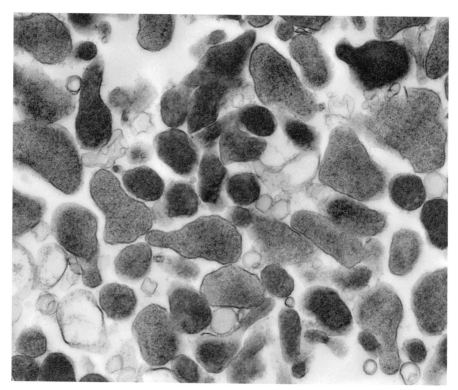

While Craig Venter and Hamilton Smith directed the group of scientists at TIGR who were sequencing the genome of *Hemophilus influenzae*, a second team, with Claire Fraser at its head, sequenced the genome of this small bacterium, *Mycoplasma genitalium*. Venter and Smith later used *M. genitalium*, which lives naturally in the human genital tract, as a template for attempts to build an artificial microorganism. *(SPL/Photo Researchers, Inc.)*

undertaking: synthesizing a complete chromosome or even perhaps a living organism from inanimate chemicals. As the first step in such a project, he arranged a collaboration between Scott Peterson, a scientist at TIGR, and Clyde A. Hutchinson of the University of North Carolina, Chapel Hill. In what they called the Minimal Life Project, the two researchers inactivated the little bacterium's genes one by one to find out which genes were necessary for survival. They found that only about 300 of the microbe's 517 genes appeared to be essential.

GROUNDBREAKING ADVANCES

Craig Venter and Hamilton Smith announced their group's sequencing achievements at the yearly meeting of the American Society of Microbiology in Washington, D.C., on May 24, 1995. The hundreds of scientists attending their talk gave them a standing ovation. "I had never seen so big and spontaneous a reaction at a scientific meeting before," Venter wrote with understandable pride in *A Life Decoded*. Besides being a ground-breaking achievement in genomics—determining a sequence almost 2 million base pairs long by putting together about 26,000 tiny pieces of DNA—the TIGR work, Venter wrote, was "the first full-fledged demonstration that the shotgun method could be used to read a whole genome." Even James Watson, Venter's old adversary, was quoted in a *New York Times* article as calling the sequencing of *Hemophilus influenzae* "a great moment in science."

Venter's team published the complete sequence of the *Hemophilus influenzae* genome, as well as the chart showing the genes' functions and relationships, in *Science* on July 28. Fraser's group printed their paper on the genome of *Mycoplasma genitalium* in the same journal on October 20. According to Venter, the *Hemophilus* paper soon became the most cited in biology. In addition to providing the first information on the organization of a whole genome, it offered a wealth of data that could help scientists understand bacteria and learn more about genes and proteins involved in key biological functions. Finally, the paper's authors stated, the whole-genome shotgun sequencing strategy that the team had used on *Hemophilus* "has potential to facilitate the sequencing of the human genome."

These two papers were not Venter's only major publications in late 1995. In September, after Venter had struggled with Haseltine for more than a year about the conditions under which the material could be used by other scientists, *Nature* published most of the ESTs from TIGR's Human Gene Anatomy Project in a special 377-page Genome Directory issue. Venter also made more than 345,000 ESTs available online in a human cDNA database. Both scientific and popular news articles praised his release of the sequences.

The dispute about the human anatomy sequences was one of many that made Venter want to distance himself and TIGR from HGS as much as possible. He had already signed over most of his HGS stock to TIGR, but he decided to sell some of the rest in late 1995. Although he wrote in *A Life Decoded* that making a personal fortune was never his aim, he was happy to find that the stock sale brought him enough money to buy the boat of his dreams—an 82-foot (25-m) yacht that cost about $1.25 million. Seeing his new genomic science as a kind of magic, he named the yacht *Sorcerer* and had the boat's sail painted with the figure of a wizard, wearing a classic pointed hat. To some eyes, the wizard bore a strong resemblance to Venter himself.

THE THIRD KINGDOM

TIGR went on to sequence more microorganisms in 1996. Surely the strangest of them was *Methanococcus jannaschii,* which can survive comfortably at temperatures of 201°F (94°C) and pressures of up to 200 atmospheres. Marine scientists had discovered this microorganism in 1982 near a chimney in the seafloor that was called a white smoker because the plume of superheated water that poured out of it, bubbling up from below the Earth's crust, was whitened by clumps of the microorganisms, which made it look as if it contained ash or smoke. Unlike almost all other organisms, this

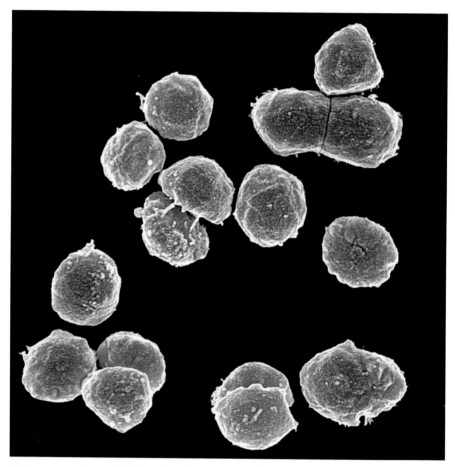

Methanococcus jannaschii, shown here, is an ocean-dwelling microorganism that can survive tremendously high temperatures and pressures. Its genome, which TIGR scientists sequenced in 1996, reveals that it is quite different from most other living things. (*B. Boonyaratanakornit and D. S. Clark, V. Vrdoljack/EM Lab, University of California, Berkeley/Visuals Unlimited, Inc.*)

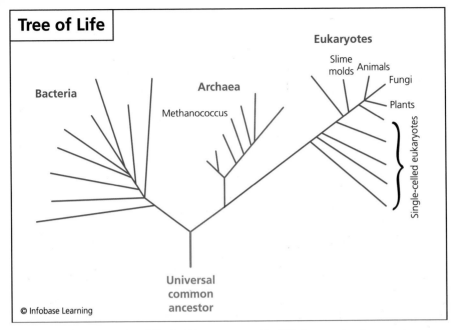

Tree of Life

Bacteria

Archaea

Methanococcus

Eukaryotes

Slime molds

Animals

Fungi

Plants

Single-celled eukaryotes

Universal common ancestor

© Infobase Learning

Carl Woese of the University of Illinois, Urbana, proposed in 1976 that certain microorganisms are so different from both bacteria (prokaryotes) and more complex organisms whose cells possess a nucleus (eukaryotes) that they deserve their own kingdom, or basic branch on the evolutionary tree of life. Woese called this kingdom the archaea, or ancient ones. Craig Venter's sequencing of the genome of one of these microbes, *Methanococcus jannaschii,* helped prove that Woese's theory was correct. This diagram shows a simplified version of the tree of life as Woese envisioned it.

microbe can live on nothing more than inorganic matter, carbon dioxide, and hydrogen.

The Department of Energy (DOE) had given TIGR a grant of $6.7 million to sequence *Methanococcus jannaschii* and certain other microorganisms. DOE was interested in this single-celled creature because it produces methane, a carbon-containing gas that can be used as a fuel, but biologists were curious about it for a more basic reason. In 1976, Carl Woese (1928–), a scientist at the Urbana campus of the University of Illinois, had proposed that certain microorganisms, including this one, are fundamentally different from all other forms of life.

Biologists traditionally had divided living things into two great kingdoms: *prokaryotes* (bacteria and other single-celled organisms whose cells do not possess nuclei) and *eukaryotes* (organisms whose cells have nuclei, including all plants and animals and some microorganisms). Woese stated that some microorganisms belong to a third kingdom, which he called the

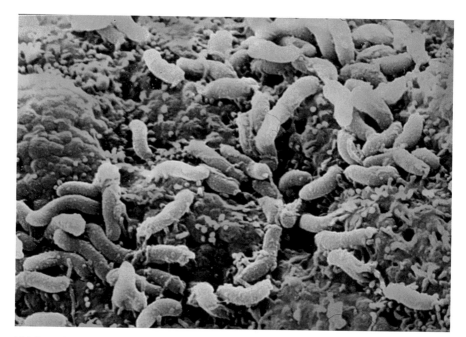

This bacterium, *Helicobacter pylori,* was one of several kinds of disease-causing bacteria whose genomes TIGR scientists sequenced in 1996. *H. pylori* can cause stomach ulcers and stomach cancer. *(Collection CNR/Phototake/Alamy)*

archaea, or ancient ones. Many scientists had rejected Woese's ideas because they redrew the accepted evolutionary tree of life so fundamentally. Venter's sequencing of *Methanococcus jannaschii,* however, revealed that Woese was right. The microbe's genome had some features in common with bacteria and some with eukaryotes, but only 44 percent of the proteins that its genes produced resembled anything known from any other kind of organism.

TIGR published the genome sequence of this bizarre microbe in *Science* in August 1996. In that same year, the TIGR scientists also sequenced the genomes of several bacteria that cause important human diseases. One was *Helicobacter pylori,* which is responsible for stomach ulcers and stomach cancer. Another was the bacterium that causes Lyme disease, a tick-borne infection that can produce joint pain and other problems.

INSTITUTIONAL DIVORCE

By mid-1997, Craig Venter felt that he and TIGR could no longer bear to remain associated with Human Genome Sciences. Wallace Steinberg, his original benefactor, had died two years previously, so no sense of loyalty constrained him. He knew he was gambling with TIGR's future in seeking this institutional separation, however, because it would mean giving up the $38 million that HGS still owed TIGR. (Steinberg had arranged for HGS to pay TIGR his promised $70 million, later raised to $85 million, over a 10-year period.) Venter believed that once TIGR was not associated with a for-profit firm NIH and other government and academic funding sources would make up the loss by offering to pay for the institute's projects—but this was by no means a certainty.

Venter later told Ingrid Wickelgren that the loss of TIGR's future revenue from HGS was "the best $38 million I ever spent" because it gave him the freedom to do what, he maintains in his autobiography, he had wanted to do all along: give his data to anyone who wanted to work on it. On the same day that the separation of TIGR and HGS became final—June 20, 1997—Venter put a vast amount of the genomic data that TIGR had gathered from both bacteria and humans onto the Internet, where it could be accessed without restriction. Doing so greatly improved his reputation with other scientists.

In spite of his wealth and his sometimes controversial approaches to science and life, Craig Venter, it seemed, was no longer a devil with horns. His classification as one of the good guys, however, would not last long.

Faster, Faster

Craig Venter and his wife celebrated the start of 1998 in high style. They were invited to the New Year Renaissance Weekend, a gathering of about 2,000 people hosted by President William and Hillary Clinton, and found themselves seated next to the Clintons at the New Year's Eve dinner. Venter wrote in *A Life Decoded* that the First Lady "was like a sponge eagerly absorbing what I had to say about the genome."

Venter knew that the year was likely to be important for him. Now that he was free of Human Genome Sciences, he had to decide what he and TIGR would do next. The Human Genome Project had made TIGR one of its six genome sequencing test centers in 1997, but it had given the institute "only token" funding, Venter wrote later in his autobiography. He felt sure that Francis Collins, still distrustful of the whole-genome shotgun technique, did not intend TIGR to be a major part of the project.

PATH TO A DREAM

If Francis Collins had doubts about Craig Venter, Stephen Lombardi, project manager at Applied Biosystems, Inc. (ABI), the maker of TIGR's invaluable DNA sequencing machines, did not share them. The day after Venter announced his separation from HGS in mid-1997, Lombardi began trying to persuade him to join forces with ABI on some kind of genome project. Venter was intrigued by the possibility of working with Mike Hunkapiller and others at the sequencer company, but he had one major concern. The Perkin-Elmer Corporation, a large business that made scientific instruments, now owned ABI, and Perkin-Elmer had a new CEO named Tony White (1948–   ), who was known for his aggressive business practices. Having just escaped from one painful relationship with a for-profit business, Venter was reluctant to enter into what he feared might become another.

The leaders of ABI became even more eager to recruit Venter as 1998 began because they had just designed a new sequencing machine that promised to be much better than the company's old ones. The hair-thin capillary tubes that this machine used for its DNA reactions were an improvement over the old machines' gels in several respects. The tubes could stand higher temperatures than the gels, which meant that more powerful electric fields could be used to move the DNA. The separation process therefore could proceed more quickly. The tubes also used smaller amounts of expensive chemical reagents and were much easier to handle than gels.

Perhaps most important, almost the entire sequencing process—loading the samples into the machine, running the DNA separations, detecting the fluorescent reactions, and cleaning out the tubes so they could be used again—could be done by robot attachments, with very little human aid. Thanks to this improved automation, each machine required only 15 minutes of human attention every 24 hours instead of the eight hours of technician time that the earlier machines had needed. The machines were also expected to produce sequences eight times faster than the old ones.

At a meeting in November 1997, one of Tony White's advisers proposed the startling idea of promoting ABI's new machines and demonstrating their power by sequencing the human genome. The Perkin-Elmer executives calculated that, using Venter's shotgun technique and about 200 of the new sequencers, they could complete the entire task in about two years. They realized that they would need someone with biological expertise to head the project, and Lombardi and Hunkapiller felt that no one could do that job better than Craig Venter himself.

Lombardi persuaded Venter and Mark Adams to fly to Foster City, California, a suburb about 25 miles (40 km) south of San Francisco, to see a prototype of the new sequencing machines in February 1998. At first, Venter calculated from the ABI group's data that even the improved machines could not work through enough DNA to sequence the huge genome in a reasonable length of time. Then, however, he realized that he had made a mathematical mistake, overestimating the number of sequences needed by ten times.

When he corrected his error, he began to feel that the feat might be possible after all . . . indeed, more than possible.

Like the Perkin-Elmer executives, Venter believed that the entire genome project could be finished in two to three years, instead of the seven years that remained for the Human Genome Project. It would cost only about a tenth as much as the federal program. Furthermore, it could be done by a single center instead of requiring many centers around the world as the HGP did. By the time he and Adams returned to Maryland, Venter wrote in *A Life Decoded*, "I had already made up my mind: I wanted to go for it. . . . There would be no better way to accelerate human medicine and science."

SELLING INFORMATION

Many questions about the private genome project remained to be settled, however. When Venter discussed the project with the Perkin-Elmer leaders a month or so later, Tony White offered to give him $300 million for the project but insisted that Venter think of a way for the company to make a profit from the endeavor. Venter warned that that profit could not come from hoarding genetic data; he wanted a written guarantee that he could publish the complete genome sequence and that anyone could access and use it without restriction.

After some consideration, Venter worked out a business plan that he hoped would meet both his needs and White's. The raw sequence data that he planned to publish—an endless list of Cs, Gs, As, and Ts—would be of little use to most researchers. However, Venter believed that he and his coworkers could arrange the information in a database that would be far easier to search—enough so that individual scientists, academic institutions, and biotechnology or pharmaceutical companies would pay to obtain access to it. According to Ingrid Wickelgren, a Perkin-Elmer board member later described the concept by saying, "We can't sell the Bible, but we can make people pay to go to church."

The database would also contain information that was not part of the human genome sequence as such. One example would be a list of variations in individual genomes that show as differences of a single base within a gene. Researchers thought there might be as many as 3 million such *single-nucleotide polymorphisms* (SNPs, pronounced "snips"). SNPs were often associated directly or indirectly with particular diseases, and James Shreeve writes that by 1998 they were "the hottest topic in medical genetics."

White would not allow the genome sequencing or the database development to take place at TIGR. Instead, he said, Perkin-Elmer would set up a

When Craig Venter set up Celera Genomics, he gave his wife, Claire Fraser (shown here in 1997), control of TIGR, his research institute. Fraser was president and director of TIGR from 1998 to 2007, after which she moved to the University of Maryland School of Medicine. She and Venter divorced in 2005. (*Jean-Christian Bourcart/Liaison Agency/Getty Images*)

new company to handle the project. Venter presented his plan for the company to Perkin-Elmer's board of directors, and they agreed to fund it on May 8. Venter, they said, would be the company's president and would receive 10 percent of its stock.

In spite of these generous terms, Venter remained uneasy about White and his corporation—and many around him were even more so. After meeting with the Perkin-Elmer legal group, Venter wrote later, his lawyer advised him to "get . . . away from them while you still can." Claire Fraser "made it clear that she thought I had taken leave of my senses" to involve himself in a situation so similar to the one he had just left. Nonetheless, Venter was so eager to fulfill his longtime dream of sequencing the human genome that he agreed to White's terms. Since he would have to leave TIGR temporarily to work with the new company, he asked Fraser to manage the institute in his absence.

A SHOCKING ANNOUNCEMENT

Craig Venter wanted to warn the genome community before Perkin-Elmer publicly announced his new venture, since the other scientists were bound to view it as competing with the Human Genome Project. He therefore met with Harold Varmus, the director of NIH, at the institutes later on May 8. Venter stressed that he saw his project as complementary to, or even a kind of collaboration with, the government effort. According to Venter's autobiography, Varmus "agreed to keep an open mind" about the subject.

Francis Collins was a good deal less accepting when Venter, Hunkapiller, and Mark Adams spoke to him still later that same day. Collins was on his way out of town, so the men met at the Red Carpet Club, the United Airlines executive lounge at Washington's Dulles Airport. The low point of that meeting came when Venter offhandedly suggested (according to James Shreeve), "While we do the human genome, you can do mouse." Collins recognized that sequencing the genome of the mouse, an animal well known in genetic science and a mammal—thus much closer in evolutionary terms to humans than any other organism whose genome had been sequenced so far—was vital so that the mouse and human genomes could be compared. Nonetheless, he found Venter's words insulting. His mood improved only a little when Hunkapiller agreed to sell ABI's new sequencing machines to the government project as well as to Venter's company.

The rest of the world heard about Venter's plans on May 10, when Nicholas Wade published a story about the new project on the front page of the Sunday *New York Times.* Wade suggested that Venter's proposed effort would be "far faster and cheaper" than the Human Genome Project. If it succeeded, he said, it would "outstrip and to some extent make redundant the government's $3 billion program to sequence the genome by 2005." The news, Ingrid Wickelgren wrote in *The Gene Masters,* struck the genomics community "like a hand grenade."

On May 11, the day after Wade's story appeared, Venter, Hunkapiller, Varmus, Collins, and Aristides (Ari) Patrinos (1949–   ), the head of the Department of Energy's portion of the Human Genome Project, held a press conference at NIH to discuss Venter's challenge and the HGP's response to it. Although Nicholas Wade had reported that Collins was considering Venter's suggestion about sequencing the mouse genome, Collins stated at the press conference that "it would be vastly premature" for the HGP to change its focus on the human at that time. The men tried to present Venter's proposal as a collaboration with the government project, but the reporters at the conference did not believe them. Most of their news stories, and others that followed, declared that the public and private projects were in a "race" to sequence the human genome.

THE HGP RESPONDS

All pretence of cooperation between the two projects vanished a few days later, when the leading scientists in the Human Genome Project attended a conference at Cold Spring Harbor. John Sulston wrote in *The Common Thread* that the researchers at the meeting "were in various stages of shock, anger, and despair." When Venter, whose talk was added to the conference at the last minute, spoke to the group on May 13, the atmosphere reminded him, as he put it in *A Life Decoded,* of "a cross between a funeral and a lynch mob."

Venter stressed in his speech that he would make all his data freely accessible, but his audience was not appeased. When he again suggested that the government project sequence the mouse genome instead of the human, Sulston's book quoted James Watson as saying, "It was like asking them to walk into the sea and drown." Several writers report that Watson compared Venter to World War II German dictator Adolf Hitler (1889–1945), claiming that "Craig wanted to own the human genome the way Hitler wanted to own the world." The genome scientists realized that their response needed to go beyond anger, however. Later in the meeting, they began to discuss the possibility of trying to produce a rough draft of the genome before Venter did.

One scientist at the meeting—Gerald Rubin (1950–) of the University of California, Berkeley—proved not to share the general hostility toward Venter. Venter wanted to sequence the genome of a smaller organism as a test run before his company took on the human, and he hoped to make arrangements for that project during the conference. While Mike Hunkapiller was describing ABI's new sequencing machines to the assembled scientists in another speech, therefore, Venter took Rubin into the hallway and asked him whether he would let Venter's company help him finish sequencing the genome of the *fruit fly.* This fly, scientifically termed *Drosophila melanogaster,* had been used in genetics experiments throughout the 20th century, and many scientists were eager to see its complete hereditary blueprint. Rubin's laboratory had been sequencing the fly genome since the early 1990s but had finished only a fifth of it.

Rubin was more interested in seeing the fruit fly sequence completed quickly than in being able to claim that achievement for himself. He recalled to John Sulston and Georgina Ferry that he told Venter, "Great, anyone who wants to help finish *Drosophila* is my friend, as long as you are going to put

THE FRUIT FLY: WORKHORSE OF GENETICS RESEARCH

Geneticists have used fruit flies *(Drosophila melanogaster)* in their experiments since shortly after the science of genetics was founded. These tiny insects are easy to attract, cheap to raise, and able to live by the thousands in even a small laboratory. They reproduce once every 10 days, producing hundreds of offspring each time, so researchers can study many fly generations in a short span of time.

Thomas Hunt Morgan (1866–1945), a geneticist at New York's Columbia University, was probably the first scientist to cultivate fruit flies in his laboratory. Morgan's laboratory, filled with the buzzing of thousands of flies (housed in used milk bottles) and the smell of the rotting bananas on which they fed, soon became known as the Fly Room.

Morgan made his first major discovery about the flies in early 1910, when he spotted a male fly that had white eyes instead of the red ones that the species usually possessed. He realized that this change must have come from a genetic mutation. He bred the strange fly to one of its red-eyed sisters and found that all their offspring had red eyes. When these offspring were mated, however, about one in four of the second-generation flies had white eyes. These results exactly matched the pattern of inheritance that the 19th-century Austrian monk Gregor Mendel (1822–84) had found for what he called dominant and recessive traits. An organism shows a *dominant trait,* or characteristic—red eyes, in this case—if it inherits even one copy of the gene for that trait. A *recessive trait* all the data in GenBank." Venter promised that he would do so, and Rubin agreed to the collaboration.

When Venter returned to the general meeting and announced his arrangement with Rubin, the genome scientists became more furious than ever. "Jim [Watson was] calling foul, Francis [Collins was] apoplectic [so angry he seemed likely to have a stroke]," and there were "mutterings that Gerry [Rubin was] collaborating with the Devil," one of the attendees, Michael Ashburner, wrote in *Won for All: How the* Drosophila *Genome Was Sequenced.*

such as white eyes, on the other hand, appears only when an organism inherits the gene for that trait from both parents.

Morgan's experiment confirmed Mendel's work, on which genetics had been built when the monk's research was rediscovered at the start of the 20th century—but it did more than that. Morgan noticed that all the white-eyed flies were male, which suggested to him that the gene for fruit fly eye color must lie on the X chromosome. Males inherit an X chromosome from their female parent and a Y chromosome from their male parent, whereas females inherit X chromosomes from both parents. A female fly would almost always have red eyes because she would be likely to receive the red eye (dominant) form of the eye color gene on one or the other of her X chromosomes. If she was the product of a mating between a red-eyed female and a white-eyed male, however, she would also have a copy of the white eye (recessive) form of the gene and would pass it on to about half of her offspring. Males who received the white eye gene on their single X chromosome would have white eyes because they would have no other copy of the gene to offset the recessive form.

Morgan's discovery was a scientific landmark because the scientists of his time had almost no idea what genes were, physically. Some researchers had suggested that they were associated with the chromosomes in the cell's nucleus, but this had been only a theory. Fruit fly eye color was the first specific trait to be tied to a particular chromosome. It greatly strengthened the evidence for a connection between chromosomes and genes.

SERIOUS DOUBTS

As with many of Craig Venter's earlier projects, the scientific community's chief question, both at the Cold Spring Harbor meeting and later, was whether a privately funded, for-profit company would really make all its data public. The Human Genome Project released its sequence data daily, whereas Venter said he would release his data only quarterly. Tony White had insisted on the delay so that his new company would have time to mine the data for DNA sequences that might be worth patenting. Venter had claimed that the company would patent only about 100 to 300 "novel gene systems," less than 1 percent of the total human genome, but this statement, too, was met with disbelief.

Many of the researchers also doubted whether Venter's whole-genome shotgun sequencing technique, successful as it had been with bacteria, could work on the human genome. James Weber of the Marshfield Clinic in Wisconsin and Eugene Myers of the University of Arizona had proposed a similar idea in 1996, but the genome scientists had rejected it. The human genome is not only many times larger than those of bacteria and other simple organisms, the critics pointed out; it also contains far more sequences in which the same string of bases appears over and over. Assembling such sequences in order would be like trying to put together a jigsaw puzzle whose picture features a cloudless blue sky or a field of flowers. So many puzzle pieces would show only blue, or nearly identical blossoms, that placing them correctly would be almost impossible.

The HGP scientists feared that there would be many spots where Venter's computers would not be able to determine the order of his project's DNA fragments. As a result, his genome sequence would contain numerous gaps. They believed that only the slower techniques that the HGP was using, which included mapping DNA sequences onto particular chromosomes, could provide a complete, accurate readout—and that full sequence, they felt, was necessary for understanding the genome. In a *New York Times* story published at the end of the Cold Spring Harbor meeting, Washington University genome scientist Robert Waterston (1943–) said that Venter's sequence would resemble "an encyclopedia ripped to shreds and scattered on the floor."

Venter admitted to reporters that his sequence would have blank spaces, but he said that he expected most of them to be in the segments of repeated DNA, which contain no genes. He also stressed that his team of scientists would sequence the genome 10 times over, which he expected to provide sufficient overlaps to close many of the gaps. He reminded everyone that other scientists had said several times before that his techniques could not possibly succeed—and they had been wrong.

A COMPANY BUILT FOR SPEED

Before Craig Venter could begin making good on his promises, he had to set up his new company. The physical location he chose for it was a pair of empty four-story buildings in Rockville, Maryland, just a mile or so from the TIGR offices. The buildings needed massive remodeling before they could house the army of sequencing machines and computers that Venter envisioned, so the dust and hammering of construction surrounded the company scientists who moved into their new home at the beginning of August.

That team included some of Venter's key employees from TIGR, such as Mark Adams, Granger Sutton, and Hamilton Smith. Venter hired many new people as well, including Eugene Myers, the computer expert from the University of Arizona who had joined James Weber in proposing to use the whole-genome shotgun method on the human genome in 1996. Myers knew Granger Sutton, and when he heard about Venter's company, he asked Sutton if he could "come and play" with the group, Venter wrote in his autobiography. Venter made Sutton and Myers the coleaders of his software development team.

Building on his lifelong love of speed, Venter also chose a name for his new enterprise: Celera (with the accent on the second syllable), which was based on a Latin word meaning "swift." The company's slogan was "Speed matters: Discovery can't wait."

Francis Collins and the other scientists of the Human Genome Project, meanwhile, were trying to decide how their program would respond to the challenge that Venter had issued in May. After talking with the many researchers who were eagerly awaiting results from the HGP, Collins found that they shared at least one goal with Venter: They cared more about obtaining the human genome sequence quickly than about having it be completely accurate. Even a sequence that contained gaps or mistakes, they explained, could help them identify genes or gene variations connected with disease and begin searches for new treatments.

This pressure, even more than the desire not to lose the so-called race between HGP and Celera, made Collins and the other HGP leaders decide in the fall that they would change the short-term goal of their project. Instead of taking the time to prepare a complete, accurate sequence, they would first create a less perfect "working draft"—which they would try to finish by the end of 2001, four years ahead of their original goal. They would then spend an additional two years bringing this sequence up to the level of accuracy that they had originally expected. They published this new schedule in an article about the project's plans in the October 23, 1998, issue of *Science*.

As Celera's "genome factory" began to take shape in the fall, its employees grew increasingly thrilled about their upcoming work. "The morale . . . was not only high, it was electric," Venter wrote in his autobiography. "People were happy, excited, and energized in a way I had never experienced before." James Shreeve added in *The Genome War* that this enthusiasm grew largely out of Venter's own. "The others took their cue from Venter, who in his confidence seemed to admit light, as if the sheen off his pate were not a reflection but a source of radiant energy of its own."

Much to Venter's irritation, Applied Biosystems had not yet sent any of the new sequencing machines it had promised. Other equipment, however, was beginning to arrive, including the company's equally impressive collection of computers. When completed, Celera's computer system would be the second largest in the world, exceeded only by one in the Department of Defense that modeled nuclear explosions.

THE PACE PICKS UP

The first of ABI's $300,000 Prism 3700 sequencers finally reached Celera on December 8, 1998. Unfortunately, most of the machines did not work properly—or, in some cases, at all. Some of the sequencers' robot arms went wild, flinging themselves across the machines and into the wall. The laser beams that were supposed to activate the dyes in the DNA samples could be equally erratic. Sometimes the machines overheated, causing the dyes to break down. Technicians who knew how to repair the balky objects were in even shorter supply than the machines themselves.

About the time the first sequencing machines arrived in Rockville, Gerald Rubin sent Celera the purified DNA for the fruit fly project. Hamilton Smith and his assistant, Cindy Pfannkoch, immediately began preparing the libraries of short DNA segments that the sequencers would analyze. They completed this work by the end of February.

The Human Genome Project was also getting ready to make the sequencing efforts that its new schedule would require. Collins and the other leaders decided that the approach the group had used thus far, in which 18 sequencing centers around the world worked on different parts of the genome, needed to be streamlined. Some of the centers could not sequence as quickly as others, or their work was of poorer quality. The leaders concluded that only the five largest, best equipped, and most experienced centers should carry out the bulk of the sequencing. They chose those centers—four in the United States and one in Britain—in February 1999.

When the heads of the five centers met shortly afterward to plan the next steps in the project, they decided to move their deadline even further forward than the one set in the fall. They wanted to hurry—and pour their sequences into GenBank as quickly as they could—not only to outrun Celera but to prevent the possibility that Venter's company would patent large stretches of the genome. They announced on March 15, 1999, that the Human Genome Project would produce a working draft covering at least 90 percent of the human genome sequence by spring 2000.

To remain in the competition, Celera also had to move up its deadline by a year. The undeclared race to sequence the human genome was picking up speed.

Photo Finish

Both Celera and the Human Genome Project (HGP) were ready to settle down to serious sequencing work in spring 1999. Celera began with the fruit fly, whereas HGP went straight to the human genome.

Craig Venter pointed out in his autobiography that since Celera and HGP by this time had the same goal in regard to the human genome (a rough draft rather than a complete, accurate sequence) and were using the same sequencing machines, the main difference between them lay in their scientific strategies. The HGP's strategy centered on *bacterial artificial chromosome (BAC) clones.* They broke up the human genome into 20,000 such clones, each about 150,000 bases long. They then shotgunned each BAC clone into many subclones. They fed each subclone into a sequencing machine, which sequenced a 500-base-pair section at one end of the subclone segment.

According to James Shreeve, Francis Collins described the public project's approach by picturing the genome as a book with many pages. The project's sequencing laboratories, Collins explained, shredded each page of the book—that is, each BAC clone—into pieces small enough for their machines to sequence, then used computer software to glue the fragments of that page back together by matching overlapping parts of the sequences. They completed the entire process for each page before going on to the next. To Venter (as he wrote in *A Life Decoded*), this so-called clone-by-clone approach meant that the government project "had thousands of mini jigsaw puzzles to

Human Genome Project's Sequencing Method

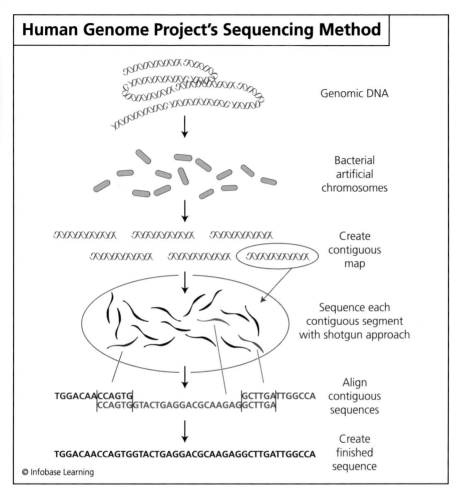

Genomic DNA

Bacterial artificial chromosomes

Create contiguous map

Sequence each contiguous segment with shotgun approach

Align contiguous sequences

Create finished sequence

TGGACAACCAGTG
CCAGTGGTACTGAGGACGCAAGAGGCTTGA
GCTTGATTGGCCA

TGGACAACCAGTGGTACTGAGGACGCAAGAGGCTTGATTGGCCA

© Infobase Learning

The Human Genome Project broke up the DNA of the human genome, chromosome by chromosome, into large segments that its scientists then inserted into bacteria, making many copies or clones of each segment. Each of these long stretches was called a bacterial artificial chromosome (BAC). Because the researchers knew approximately where on each human chromosome each BAC had originated, they could make a kind of map of the segments. They then broke up each BAC into many subclones and sequenced each of these with the shotgun method, the same technique that Craig Venter's Celera Genomics used. Finally, the scientists used the mapping information that they had obtained earlier to help them reassemble the sequenced fragments in the correct order.

solve, order, and orient." Celera, by contrast, planned to use (on both the fly and the human genomes) the whole-genome shotgun approach that Venter and Smith had pioneered with the *Hemophilus influenzae* genome. It performed each process—breaking up the original DNA, growing libraries of

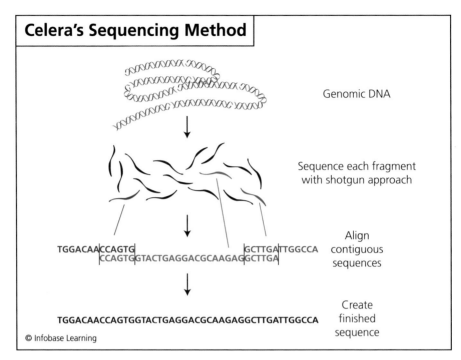

Celera's Sequencing Method

Genomic DNA

Sequence each fragment
with shotgun approach

Align
contiguous
sequences

TGGACAACCAGTG
CCAGTGGTACTGAGGACGCAAGAGGCTTGA
GCTTGATTGGCCA

Create
finished
sequence

TGGACAACCAGTGGTACTGAGGACGCAAGAGGCTTGATTGGCCA

© Infobase Learning

The main difference between the Human Genome Project's method of sequencing the human genome and Celera's was that Celera did not use an intermediate, mapping stage. Instead, it applied the shotgun sequencing technique to the entire genome at once, breaking the genome into many small fragments. After the fragments were sequenced, Celera used a specially designed computer program to assemble all of its sequences at once. This approach saved time, but it potentially made the final assembly task more difficult. Celera also used this approach when sequencing the genomes of the fruit fly and other organisms.

DNA fragments in bacteria, sequencing, and assembling—only once, on all the material from the genome.

SEQUENCING THE FRUIT FLY GENOME

Celera began sequencing the fruit fly genome in April. By this time, the company had about 100 of the 300 sequencing machines it ultimately planned to possess, though by no means all of them were working. The sequencing process started in the picking room, which held the libraries of DNA-containing bacterial colonies that Hamilton Smith and Cindy Pfannkoch had prepared. Robot arms with TV cameras attached scanned the colonies, ignoring any that overlapped. Selecting at random from the separated colonies, the arms used metal probes to pick up a tiny sample of bacteria from each chosen colony and transfer it to one of 364 small wells on a tray. The bacteria grew further in the wells for a short time, after which the trays were spun in a centrifuge to break open the bacteria and release their DNA cargo. Technicians purified the DNA and added four fluorescent dyes, each attached to a different type of false nucleotide, and then transferred the trays to the sequencers.

Every sequencer held four trays. A robot arm on the sequencer filled the machine's approximately 100 hair-thin glass capillary tubes with a reddish substance that took the place of the gel in the Sanger process. The arm then transferred DNA from one of the wells on the trays to each tube. Next, the machine ran the DNA polymerase and electric-current reactions in all the tubes at once, spreading the DNA fragments through the red material. As each fragment reached the end of its tube, a laser activated the dyes attached to its last base. A small TV camera detected the dyes and sent signals to a computer, which translated the data into a

Nini Tint, a technician, loads DNA samples into an automated sequencing machine at Celera Genomics in 2001. Automated sequencers made it possible for both Celera and the Human Genome Project (which used identical machines) to sequence the 6 billion base pairs that make up the human genome. *(AP Images)*

Automated DNA Sequencing

1. Robot arm randomly selects sample from bacterial colonies in DNA library

Robot arm — Metal probe — Bacterial colonies

2. Robot places sample in well on tray

3. Machine adds false nucleotides with fluorescent dyes to sample

4. Robot arm in sequencer puts DNA sample into capillary tube

5. Double-stranded DNA fragments of different lengths form in tube

AGATTC __ New strand
TCTAAG ⁔ Original strand
GCT
CGA   GACGTAGTCA
         CTGCATCAGT

6. As electric current draws fragments to end of tube, laser activates dyes in fragments; camera detects dye pattern and sends this information to a computer

GCTA
CGAT   Laser
CAGTTAC   light
GTCAATG   Camera

7. Computer translates dye pattern into sequence of about 500 base pairs

AGACT
TCTGA

Computer

© Infobase Learning

Automated sequencers using capillary tubes rather than gels were at the heart of the factory-like DNA sequencing operations at Celera Genomics. This diagram shows the steps in the sequencing process. The reddish polymer in the machine's hair-thin capillary tubes took the place of the unwieldy gels that older sequencers had used.

sequence of about 500 base pairs for each sample. Meanwhile, the robot cleaned out the tubes and refilled them with different DNA samples for another run.

On a different floor of the Celera gene factory, Eugene Myers and his fellow computer experts were designing a multistage program that would—they hoped—reassemble the sequenced segments in order. The first stage of the assembler program screened out contaminating sequences from the bacteria in which the DNA had been cloned. The second stage checked the remaining sequences against sequences from the fly genome that Rubin's group had already worked out.

Next, a part of the program that the group called the Overlapper compared every sequence to every other. When the Overlapper identified two overlapping fragments, it assembled them into a tentative contig. (Pieces were considered to overlap if they shared at least 50 base pairs.) The scientists knew that the fruit fly genome contains many repeated sequences, so many fragments potentially could overlap with more than one other fragment. To avoid this problem, another part of the program termed the Unitigger eliminated all such sequences, keeping only the *unitigs,* or sequences that could be overlapped with only a single other sequence. The Unitigger kept adding fragments to existing unitigs until it hit a point at which one end of a unitig could be matched with more than one other fragment. When this occurred, it put the unitig aside and eventually broke it up again for rematching.

Unlike HGP, which sequenced only one end of each of its DNA segments, Celera sequenced *both* ends of each segment that it ran through its machines. Smith and Pfannkoch had used only segments either 2,000 or 10,000 base pairs long in their libraries, so the assembler program had a mate pair of sequences for each segment that were a known distance apart. The final stage of Myers's program, the Scaffolder, checked the unitigs to see which contained sequences that had been identified as coming from opposite ends of the same segment. If the sequence of one mate in a pair matched the end of one unitig, and the other half of the pair uniquely duplicated the end of another unitig, the two unitigs were almost sure to be next to each other in the genome, and the program could join them. In this way, it assembled the unitigs into larger chains called *scaffolds.* Not all the scaffolds could be linked, and some base pairs within them would still be unknown, but Myers believed that his program's procedure was good enough to assemble a fairly complete and accurate genome.

Eugene Myers and other computer experts at Celera Genomics created a complex program that joined thousands of sequenced DNA fragments together to make a complete genome. Here, analyst Mark Goodwin works with one of the many computers in Celera's support center in 2001. *(AP Images)*

MANAGEMENT TENSIONS

While Celera's technicians were struggling with balky sequencers and its programmers were wrestling with awkward computer code, Craig Venter was—as always—arguing with Tony White. White had sold Perkin-Elmer's original analytical instruments division in April and renamed the remaining company the PE Corporation. After HGP announced its new deadline in March, White and the other PE executives forbade Venter to issue Celera's human data quarterly, as he had promised the HGP scientists he would do. Venter protested, and White compromised by saying that Venter could post the data on the company's Web site, where scientists could search it but could not download it.

Venter realized that part of White's insistence came from the need to please Amgen, Novartis, and Pharmacia Upjohn, the three large drug companies that had signed up for Celera's database service in the first half of 1999. The companies would not want to pay between $5 and $9 million a year for information that others could obtain for free. Venter, however, still believed that his business plan could succeed without having to limit access to raw data.

Venter's outspokenness and fondness for talking to journalists were another subject of contention between him and White. White said he was afraid that some of Venter's public statements, particularly those that criticized the Human Genome Project, would hurt the value of Celera's stock. Venter wrote in his autobiography, however, that he believed White was also personally jealous of the seemingly endless publicity that Venter received. If this was true, the display of pictures and articles about himself that Venter placed prominently in the hallway leading to his office cannot have improved White's feelings.

Although Venter's scientific team was still immersed in the fruit fly project, Venter himself was starting to think about the larger task ahead. For one thing, he needed to decide whose DNA Celera was going to sequence when it turned to the human genome. Samples from several people would need to be used, so that the sequence would represent both men and women and would cover different racial groups. Eugene Myers calculated that five or six samples would introduce enough variation to make the genome reasonably representative. The team planned to obtain most of their sequence from a single individual and determine partial sequences for the rest.

Celera planned to keep the names of its DNA donors secret, but the donors could face problems if their identity leaked out. If their genomes proved to include genes associated with a high risk of developing a disease, they might have trouble obtaining health or life insurance, for instance. Law required the company to spell out these risks for prospective donors and have them sign a form showing that they had given their *informed consent* to the use of their DNA.

Obtaining informed consent might be tricky, but Venter knew of one person whose consent could be assured. In a move that would cause both controversy and amusement when it was revealed several years later, he decided that the main sample of DNA Celera sequenced would be his own. Hamilton Smith provided another sample, and three women, who have remained anonymous—one African-American, one Hispanic, and one Chinese—contributed the remaining ones. Smith began building DNA libraries from these five samples in July 1999.

PREVENTING DISCRIMINATION: GENETIC INFORMATION NONDISCRIMINATION ACT (GINA) OF 2008

Scientists and biotechnology companies used information about the human genome to develop a number of genetic tests during the 2000s. Some tests detect genes that cause inherited illnesses, but most focus on gene variations that (as far as researchers know now) simply increase a person's risk of suffering from a condition such as cancer or heart disease. Other genes or factors in the person's lifestyle or environment may offset that risk and keep him or her from actually developing the disease.

As the number of genetic tests increased and more people began to use them, fears of discrimination also grew. Health and life insurance companies can deny insurance or charge higher premiums to people who have *preexisting conditions*—medical conditions they developed before applying for the insurance. Because employers frequently pay for at least part of their workers' health insurance, they are unlikely to hire people who have been ill or seem likely to become so and may therefore generate higher insurance costs. People were afraid that a genetic predisposition to a disease would be counted as a preexisting condition and therefore would make obtaining jobs or insurance difficult. This fear made them either avoid genetic tests entirely or take them secretly so that employers and insurance companies would not learn the tests' results.

In 2008, Congress passed the *Genetic Information Nondiscrimination Act (GINA)*, a law designed to protect citizens against genetic discrimination. GINA forbids health insurers to deny insurance coverage or charge higher rates to a healthy person because of a genetic predisposition to a disease. Similarly, employers may not use genetic information to decide whether to hire, fire, promote, or pay an individual. The law does not affect life, disability, or long-term care insurance.

Thanks to GINA, people should no longer be afraid to take genetic tests. The law also benefits researchers in medical genetics, who often had trouble persuading people to donate DNA for experimental analysis (as Craig Venter feared might happen with the human genome samples) because of concerns about what the experiments might reveal. GINA recognizes that, although genes are important in determining a person's health, it is not fair to judge health on the basis of genes alone.

ANNOTATION JAMBOREE

Eugene Myers and his computer group faced what looked like a disaster when they first tried to assemble the almost-completed fruit fly genome sequence at the end of August: Their assembler program failed miserably. Through two weeks of sleepless days and nights, the team searched frantically for the source of the problem. They finally traced it to an error in a single one of the 150,000 lines of computer code that made up the program. The error made the program discard huge numbers of matched fragments that in fact were unitigs and should have been used. After correcting this mistake, the group retested the program, and it worked perfectly.

The fruit fly project was now essentially complete. The last segment of the fly genome was sequenced on September 8, and Myers's computer program had no further trouble arranging the thousands of segments in order. Venter, Adams, Myers, and Rubin announced their triumph at the Genomic Sequencing and Analysis Conference on September 17. "The applause was loud, long, and sincere," Venter wrote in *A Life Decoded.*

Venter and the others knew that obtaining the fly genome sequence was just the beginning of the work to be done. The next stage was *annotation*—analyzing the sequence with pattern-finding software to identify genes and other useful information, such as similarities to genes already known in other organisms. Such work potentially could take at least a year, but the Celera scientists wanted to carry it out quickly so they could move on to the human genome. Rubin, Venter, and Adams therefore decided to approach the task in a new way. In November 1999, they held a 10-day annotation jamboree, where they invited about 50 top *Drosophila* specialists from around the world to come to Celera, examine the fruit fly sequence on computers, and brainstorm ideas about it together.

The jamboree was a tremendous success. James Shreeve called it a "coordinated frenzy of discovery." Many of the scientists skipped meals or ate in front of their computer screens and worked late into the night, too thrilled to waste time eating or sleeping. One researcher told Venter that the experience was "like going into outer space or underneath the sea." Another said that the attending scientists were making "more exciting discoveries in a few hours than they had in their entire careers."

One of the group's most startling findings was that the fly had only about 13,600 genes—fewer than the 18,000 genes of the little roundworm *Caenorhabditis elegans,* another favorite animal of geneticists whose genome had recently been sequenced, even though the worm has only a tenth as many cells as the fly. Only 2,500 of those genes had been known before

Celera's work. Among the new genes were a number that matched known human genes, including several genes involved in diseases.

MUD WRESTLING

The leaders of Celera and the Human Genome Project continued to clash. Scientists both within and outside the groups tried several times in 1998 and 1999 to set up a collaboration between the two, but the efforts always failed. The rival scientists' views on key issues such as the release of data and the patenting of genetic information were simply too far apart for compromise to be possible. For instance, Collins and the other HGP leaders believed that genome data should be posted in GenBank or a similar open database as soon as it was generated, but Venter and Tony White maintained that such a policy did not make business sense for a private, for-profit company like Celera. They planned to make their data available for scientific use without charge, but they wanted to wait a year before depositing it in Genbank so that rival database companies could not simply download their material, repackage it, and resell it.

On the other hand, Venter saw nothing wrong with making use of the data that the HGP published, adding it to the sequences Celera obtained with its own army of machines. In early 2000, he asked Eugene Myers to modify Celera's computer program so that it could incorporate the public project's sequences. The only problem with doing this, Venter and Myers found, was that much of the HGP data was less accurate than Celera's. Myers concluded that the only way he could use the data without reducing his assembly program's effectiveness was to ignore the government's mapping information. He therefore told the program to shred the HGP's assembled BAC clone sequences into 500-base-pair pieces and treat them just like the random fragments that came from Celera's own sequencing machines. Myers called his new program Grande, in honor of the giant coffee drinks that he and his fellow workers consumed while they were developing it.

As an alternative to Grande, Myers's team created a second program, Overlayer, that *did* take advantage of the HGP's mapping data. It matched Celera's sequences to those of the government project's individual BAC clones as best it could, in essence sorting all of the Celera data into 20,000 separate piles, and then ran the assembler on each pile separately. Overlayer, however, did not work well because the errors in the public data kept the computer from making clear matches between fragments.

Relations between the private and public genome projects sank to a new low during the first part of 2000. On February 28, HGP leaders and the

Wellcome Trust, the charity that funded most of Britain's contribution to the genome project, sent a four-page letter to Celera. The letter stated their grievances against the company and warned that all possibility of collaboration between the two projects would end if Celera did not agree to the other groups' terms for data release by March 6. Then, on March 5, without waiting for the letter's deadline, the Wellcome Trust leaked the letter to the *Los Angeles Times*, which published it on the newspaper's front page. If this tactic was meant to increase pressure on Celera, it failed; it simply made Venter furious. In recounting the story, Justin Gillis, a reporter for the *Washington Post*, wrote, "More and more, the Human Genome Project, supposedly one of mankind's noblest undertakings, is resembling a mud-wrestling match."

ROLLER COASTER SPRING

The leaked letter soon became the least of Celera's worries. Buoyed by general enthusiasm about biotechnology and the scientific achievements of Celera and HGP, the price of Celera's stock and that of other biotechnology companies rose rapidly in late 1999 and early 2000. The value of Venter's personal shares, at least on paper, rose to the astounding sum of $700 million. On March 14, however, President Clinton and British prime minister Tony Blair (1953–   ) issued a joint statement at a press conference saying that the "raw, fundamental data of the human genome, including the human DNA sequence and its variations, should be made freely available to scientists everywhere." Investors interpreted this statement as meaning that the president disapproved of gene patenting and might even be planning to restrict or disallow it. Biotechnology stocks in general, and Celera stock in particular, therefore plummeted in the market. Venter alone lost $300 million. A clarification issued a day later, saying that Clinton did not intend to restrict patenting, did little to improve the financial picture.

Venter's concern about these developments was offset by the warm reception he received at an annual conference of fruit fly scientists in Philadelphia on March 23. The organizers of the conference had invited him to give its keynote lecture, and those who attended the lecture found a CD-ROM containing the fly genome sequence waiting on every seat. After hearing Venter's talk, the assembled scientists gave him a long standing ovation. The next day, the Venter group's three papers about the fly genome appeared in *Science*. Venter says these papers became "some of the most cited scientific papers in history."

Venter was also cheered by Gerald Rubin's comments about their collaboration at the annual meeting of the American Association for the Advancement of Science the preceding month. "Working with Celera has been one of the most pleasurable scientific experiences in my thirty-year career," Rubin had said. "Seldom have I encountered a group of individuals who were so dedicated and so hard working. . . . They have behaved with the highest standards of personal integrity and scientific rigor. . . . [Venter] always has kept his promises."

PIZZA DIPLOMACY

By the beginning of April, both Celera and the Human Genome Project had (or at least were claiming they had) almost completed their rough draft of the human genome sequence. Each was doing everything in its power to make sure that its rival did not announce that achievement first. Embarrassed and disturbed by the highly publicized quarreling between the leaders of the two projects, President Clinton bluntly told his science adviser, Neal Lane, on April 7, "Fix it. . . . Make these guys work together."

Neither Lane nor anyone else had any idea how to accomplish this task, however, until the Department of Energy (DOE)'s Aristides Patrinos stepped in. Patrinos not only lived near Venter and Francis Collins but had been friends with both men for years. He set up several private meetings between the two at his home in May, during which he persuaded them to talk over their differences as they snacked on pizza and beer. (A story in *Time* magazine later called Patrinos's peacemaking "pizza diplomacy.") Under Patrinos's gentle pressure, the rivals finally agreed to take part in a joint announcement of the rough draft completion. Patrinos promised that President Clinton would also participate.

The White House set the date of the announcement as June 26. This put tremendous pressure on both projects, neither of which was sure it could have a complete sequence that soon. After nightmarish around-the-clock efforts by their computer departments, the two groups finished their sequences mere days before the scheduled announcement. John Sulston admitted in *The Common Thread*, "We [both sides] just put together what we did have and wrapped it up in a nice way, and said it was done."

A TRIUMPHANT TIE

Craig Venter did not sleep during the night before the White House ceremony, he wrote in *A Life Decoded*. As he dressed for the historic event, he said, "I was . . . determined that this was going to be my day, perhaps one of the most important in my life."

Venter and Francis Collins walked with President Clinton to the East Room of the White House at a little after 10 A.M. Clinton began his remarks by recalling that explorer Meriwether Lewis (1774–1809) had presented a new map of the Louisiana Purchase, which extended the territory of the United States to the western border of North America, to President Thomas Jefferson (1743–1826) in that same room almost two centuries earlier. Now, the president said,

> the world is joining us here . . . to behold a map of even greater significance. We are here to celebrate the completion of the first survey of the entire human genome. Without a doubt, this is the most important, most wondrous map ever produced by humankind.

Clinton went on to refer to "the robust and healthy competition" that had led to that achievement.

In a ceremony held in the East Room of the White House on June 26, 2000, Craig Venter (left), President Bill Clinton, and Francis Collins celebrated the completion of a rough draft of the sequence of the human genome, which Clinton called "the most wondrous map ever produced by humankind." This ceremony gave Venter, head of Celera Genomics, and Collins, head of the government-sponsored Human Genome Project, credit for having finished their respective sequences at essentially the same time, ending the bitter competition between the two projects. (AP Images)

Prime Minister Tony Blair next made a speech, broadcast live by satellite from Britain and shown on two huge plasma television screens in the White House room. Francis Collins spoke third, praising Celera's "elegant and innovative strategy . . . highly complementary to the approach taken by the public project." He concluded, "I'm happy that today the only race we are talking about is the human race."

Venter spoke last. Just as Collins and the others had praised him, he praised them. "The [human] genome sequence," he said, "represents a new starting point for science and medicine, with potential impact on every disease." He ended his speech with these words:

> Some have said to me that sequencing the human genome will diminish humanity by taking the mystery out of life. Poets have argued that genome sequencing is an example of sterilizing reductionism that will rob them of their inspiration. Nothing could be further from the truth. The complexities and wonder of how the inanimate chemicals that are our genetic code give rise to the imponderables of the human spirit should keep poets and philosophers inspired for millennia.

Venter knew that he, too, would go on being inspired by the genomes of humans and other organisms for many years to come.

Exploring the World, Saving the World

The truce between Celera Genomics and the Human Genome Project, so joyfully celebrated at the White House on June 26, lasted "about as long as it takes a television crew to pack up its gear," James Shreeve wrote in *The Genome War*. As part of that truce, the two groups had agreed to publish papers about their genome sequences in the same scientific journal at the same time. By fall 2000, however, bitter disagreements had erupted about the terms under which that publication would occur.

DISPUTES ABOUT ACCESS

The project leaders decided that their groundbreaking papers would appear in *Science*. The complete base sequence of the human genome was far too long to publish in the magazine itself, so both groups planned to post their sequences on the Internet. The Human Genome Project would put its sequence into GenBank, while Celera would publish its sequence on its own Web site.

Science normally requires its authors to make supporting information for their papers freely available, but Venter and other Celera executives insisted that that was not practical in their case. After discussion with the magazine's editors, they agreed that anyone could search the sequence on the site or request a DVD containing the complete sequence without restrictions. Academic researchers could also download one megabase (1 million base pairs, about 0.03 percent of the total human code) per week simply by clicking on an agreement not to sell or redistribute the information. If they wished to download more than that, a representative of their institution had to make the same promise in writing. For-profit businesses would have to pay to access the sequence or else promise not to use its data commercially. These restrictions were necessary, Celera officials said, to prevent the company's business competitors from downloading its information and reselling it as their own.

The *Science* editors decided that Celera's requirements were reasonable and agreed to publish the Venter group's paper on those terms. The Human Genome Project leaders, however, felt that the restrictions set a precedent that could dangerously limit the circulation of scientific information. In *The Common Thread,* John Sulston points out that Celera's ban on republishing its data, for instance, meant that the data could not be put into public genome databases. This isolation would make it hard for scientists to search multiple databases at once for human sequences.

As a protest against *Science*'s cooperation with Celera, the HGP leaders sent their paper to the rival journal *Nature* instead. That magazine published the HGP paper on February 15, 2001, and *Science* printed the Celera paper a day later. Both papers included a preliminary analysis of the genome. (The Celera paper featured a five-foot- [1.5-m] high foldout map of the genome, showing gene families with different functions in different colors.) "Seeing the *Science* paper in print gave me one of the most intense feelings of satisfaction I have ever experienced," Craig Venter wrote in *A Life Decoded.*

DISPUTES ABOUT ACCURACY

For a while, the two teams' behind-the-scenes bitterness was swallowed up in the scientific community's excitement at beholding the "book of instructions" for human life for the first time. Refining and detailed analysis of the sequences would take years, but several startling facts were clear immediately. Perhaps the most surprising was that the human genome appeared to contain far fewer genes than anyone had predicted. Scientists had estimated that humans had 80,000 to 100,000 genes, but the actual number now seemed to be only 26,000 to 40,000—just a little more than 1 percent of the total DNA sequence. Genome scientists speculated that humans can survive with such a small number of genes because each gene is able to make several different proteins, rather than only a single protein as genes in simpler organisms do.

Bad feeling between the two rival scientific teams soon erupted once more. Both groups had admitted from the beginning that their sequences contained many gaps—but each team claimed that its sequence was of better quality than its competitor's. Several HGP leaders published papers criticizing Celera's sequence and whole-genome shotgun technique in 2001, claiming that Celera would not have had a publishable sequence at all if it had not used data from the government project. (Celera's *Science* paper described versions of the sequence obtained with both the Grande and the Overlayer programs, but the sequence that the company put on its Web site was the Overlayer one, because it was 2 percent more complete. This was the version that used the HGP mapping data.)

Venter's group vigorously defended its work. For instance, they pointed out that the long-awaited sequence of the mouse genome that they completed by the end of 2000 and published on April 27, 2001, was based entirely on data that Celera had obtained with the whole-genome shotgun method. They said that this sequence contained more pieces arranged in a linear sequence and had considerably fewer gaps than either published version of the human genome sequence. In June 2001, furthermore, Granger Sutton told a meeting of computer scientists from both projects that Celera had resequenced the human genome using only its own data and produced a sequence more accurate than either sequence they had described in *Science*. Sutton invited any interested scientists to come to Celera and examine the sequence for themselves.

LEAVING CELERA

Celera's database business was finally starting to show a profit. The database had gained many new subscribers after the company sequenced the human genome, including Harvard University, the University of California system, the Howard Hughes Medical Institute (the largest philanthropic organization supporting biomedical research in the United States), the government of Australia, and even the National Institutes of Health. These institutions were eager to see not only the human genome sequence but that of the mouse genome, which Celera offered to its subscribers a year and a half before the Human Genome Project published its own mouse sequence. By late 2001, Ingrid Wickelgren writes, database subscriptions were bringing in $100 million a year.

Nonetheless, the business apparently was not as profitable as the shareholders of the parent company, now called Applera (from a combination of

Applied Biosystems and *Celera*), had hoped. In 2001, therefore, Tony White and the other Applera leaders decided to change Celera's direction. Rather than concentrating on gene sequencing and databases, they said, the company would focus on the study of proteins and on drug development.

Venter cooperated with the change at first, but it made him increasingly uneasy. He wrote in his autobiography that he began thinking of leaving Celera in late 2001. White and the Applera executives did not wait for him to do so, however. On January 21, 2002, the Applera board of directors voted unanimously to fire Venter. Their press release stated that they had let Venter go because he had no experience in drug design, but Venter later claimed that their real motives grew out of the longstanding bad feeling between him and White and the belief that he had failed to make enough profit for the parent company. The executives insisted that Venter leave Celera immediately, not even giving him a chance to say good-bye to the other scientists with whom he had worked so hard.

CHANGING COURSE

As he often did when he was under stress, Craig Venter turned to the sea for comfort after he was forced out of Celera. In December 2000, he had bought a new yacht, the *Sorcerer II,* and he took it on an extended sailing trip in the Caribbean while he recovered from the shock of his firing and tried to decide what to do next. He considered returning to TIGR, but Claire Fraser made it clear that she had no desire to give up the institute that she had now controlled for several years.

Venter also soothed his feelings of rejection with the memory that in 2001 and 2002 he had finally begun to receive the recognition as a scientist that he had craved so badly. Among others, during those years he won the King Faisal International Prize for Science, the World Health Award, the Paul Ehrlich and Ludwig Darmstaedter Prize, the Takeda Award, and the Gairdner Award. In May 2002, he was also elected to the U.S. National Academy of Sciences, a great honor.

Venter was seldom either discouraged or silent for long, and this period was no exception. On April 27, he returned to the headlines by revealing to the *New York Times* that most of the composite genome that Celera had sequenced was his own. Venter insisted in his autobiography that "the reason for this choice was a matter of science, not ego or hubris." In an interview published in *BioITWorld* in November 2002, he said that using his own genome was partly a matter of leadership in a time when many people refused to take genetic tests because they feared that information uncovered in such tests would be used against them. He added, "I was [also] a donor out of just absolute scientific curiosity. My view is, how can anybody possibly work in this field and not want to know their genetic code?"

A few days later, Venter announced that he was using $100 million from the sale of his shares of Celera and other stocks to establish three new organizations: The Center for the Advancement of Genomics (whose initials, by no coincidence, were TCAG, the letters that stand for the four bases in DNA), the Institute for Biological Energy Alternatives (IBEA), and the J. Craig Venter Science Foundation, which would fund the other two. He also set up a new sequencing facility large enough to rival Celera's, which the institutes would share with TIGR.

SYNTHESIZING LIFE

Craig Venter said that TCAG would be a public policy institute, designed to help opinion makers and the general public understand the implications of scientists' new discoveries about human genetic code. His plans for IBEA, however, were more startling. They grew out of the *Mycoplasma genitalium* "minimal life project" that Scott Peterson and Clyde Hutchinson had carried out in 1995, when Venter was still at TIGR. Venter hoped he could synthesize the string of about 300 genes that Peterson and Hutchinson had found to be essential for the little microbe's survival and use it as a template to create new microorganisms. Using genetic engineering, he wanted to give these microorganisms abilities that could improve the environment, such as the power to use solar energy, water, and the greenhouse gas carbon dioxide to make hydrogen fuel.

Venter seldom let anything stop him from carrying out a new idea, but the thought of creating life "from scratch" had given even him pause. At the time of the minimal life project, he asked a group of ethicists and religious leaders whether making a new organism in this way would be morally acceptable. The panel concluded in 1999 that there was nothing wrong with the project as Venter had described it, but Venter had become involved with Celera and the sequencing of the human genome by that time, so he put his plans for synthetic life aside. Now he was eager to take them up again.

Venter was not the only one who believed that synthetically created microbes might help the environment. In November 2002, at the urging of Venter's old friend Ari Patrinos, the Department of Energy (DOE) awarded IBEA $3 million to begin the process of sequencing microorganisms that could be used to make nonpolluting fuel or improve the environment in other ways. DOE gave IBEA an additional $9 million in spring 2003.

MASS SEQUENCING

Making a synthetic microbe with genes able to carry out particular tasks would be much easier if scientists could model it on microorganisms that performed those feats naturally. Partly in the hope of detecting such microorganisms, in early 2003 Venter launched a second new project almost as ambitious as the one of synthesizing life: shotgun-sequencing the genomes of microorganisms in water samples from the world's oceans. He believed that learning exactly what microbes live in the oceans would help scientists understand and monitor global warming's effects on sea life, and he hoped that such knowledge would produce new tools to combat those effects as well. In sequencing the genomes of many different microorganisms at the same time and using the results to attempt to understand the creatures' ecological relationship to one another, Venter helped to establish a new scientific field called *metagenomics* or *environmental genomics,* the study of evolution and ecology at the genome level.

As with so many of Venter's earlier projects, many scientists thought his plan could not possibly succeed. Some of the microbe sequencing projects that Venter and the other scientists had carried out at TIGR in the mid-1990s, however, had convinced him that computer programs could assemble multiple small genomes at the same time and separate them afterward. He tested his idea by breaking the sequences of all the microbial genomes known at the time (about 100) into short stretches of DNA, then running all the fragments through his assembler program at once. The program put the genomes together correctly. Even so, doubters questioned whether the procedure would work on random samples of ocean water.

THE OCEAN'S GENOME

Just as Craig Venter and his fellow scientists at Celera had sequenced the fruit fly genome as a pilot project to test and prove their techniques before beginning the much greater task of sequencing the human genome, Venter began his world ocean venture with a test project that involved a single, relatively small body of water called the Sargasso Sea. Venter chose this sea, a branch of the Atlantic Ocean off Bermuda, because its hot, motionless water was thought to lack nutrients that most marine organisms need. As a result, biologists believed that the sea was the oceanic equivalent of a desert, containing very few forms of life.

A team of researchers from IBEA collected samples of water from six sites in the Sargasso Sea in February and May 2003. They ran each sample through a set of filters with increasingly small openings to extract the microorganisms (including viruses) within it, then froze the DNA-coated filters and sent them back to the Venter Foundation's new sequencing center. Scientists at the center applied the shotgun sequencing procedure to all of the DNA on each filter as a unit, as if it had come from a single organism, even though it represented millions of different microbes. At the end of the sequencing, the assembler program separated the results into individual genomes and genome fragments. Other software scanned the sequences for known genes and grouped the genes according to their functions. The result was what Venter called "a snapshot of the microbial diversity in a single drop of seawater—a genome of the ocean itself."

The research group published the results of their expedition in *Science* on April 2, 2004. The Sargasso Sea, they said, was anything but a desert when examined at the microscopic level. They had found at least 1,800 new species of microorganisms and more than 1.2 million new genes—about as many genes as had been identified up to that time for all organisms put together—in a mere 53 gallons (200 L) of seawater. Some 800 of those genes were involved in converting sunlight into energy and thus might be useful in creating fuel that humans could use.

Like so many of Craig Venter's other projects, the Sargasso Sea voyage aroused controversy. No longer constrained by commercial ties, Venter placed the genome sequences of the microbes he sampled in GenBank as soon as they were available. A Canadian environmentalist group called the Action Group on Erosion, Technology, and Concentration (ETC Group), however, complained that he should not have done so. The microorganisms came from water belonging to Bermuda, they said, so the microbes' genes in essence belonged to Bermuda as well. By publishing the genetic sequences, Venter made it impossible for that country to patent the genes and was thereby cheating the Bermudan people. Venter later complained to science reporter David Ewing Duncan (who quoted him in *The Geneticist Who Played Hoops with My DNA*) about the irony that he was being criticized for making genome data public—the very thing that the Human Genome Project scientists had wanted him to do.

Well before the results of the Sargasso venture appeared in print, Venter decided that the pilot project was "a winner," as he wrote in *A Life Decoded*,

Path of the *Sorcerer II* Expedition

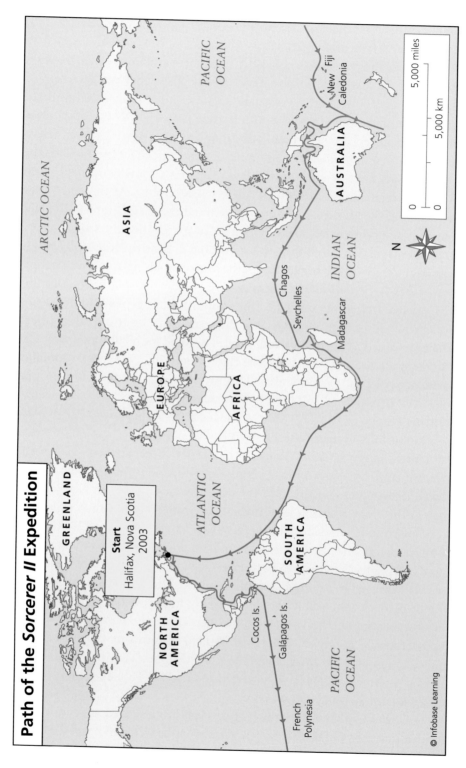

© Infobase Learning

and launched a much larger venture with the same purpose. The *Sorcerer II* expedition, as he called it, departed from Halifax, Nova Scotia, Canada, in August 2003. He planned for the ship, now refitted to be a floating laboratory as well as a luxury yacht, to spend the next two years sailing through the world's oceans.

The *Sorcerer II* sailed down the eastern coasts of North and Central America, through the Panama Canal, and into the tropical Pacific. The scientists in its crew took a sample of the surface water every 200 nautical miles (370 km) and recorded the temperature, pH (acidity), salinity (saltiness), wind speed, and wave height at that spot. They then filtered the sample, extracted the DNA from the filtered material, froze it, and sent it to Venter's sequencing center. Sometimes Venter himself carried the precious cargo, since he flew out to visit the expedition frequently. A crew from television's Discovery Channel also went along to film parts of the journey.

THE GENESIS PROJECT

When Craig Venter was not helping the *Sorcerer II* team investigate the world's waters, he was directing other researchers on the synthetic genome project, which he called the Genesis Project. Hamilton Smith, who (along with a number of other scientists) had followed Venter from Celera, and Clyde Hutchinson, one of the scientists from the old Minimal Life Project, led the team that carried out this program. In November 2003, the group announced that they had synthesized a virus called phi-X174 from 259 *oligonucleotides*. They showed that the virus could infect bacteria and reproduce inside them, just as the natural virus does. They were not the first to synthesize a virus; researchers at the State University of New York, Stony Brook, had announced their synthesis of the virus that causes polio in the summer of 2002. The SUNY project, however, had taken three years, whereas Venter's group made their virus in just two weeks.

Like several other scientific papers about synthesizing or modifying viruses written during this period, Venter's paper raised potential national security issues. In the wake of the attack on New York's World Trade Center on September 11, 2001, government officials around the world, and

(opposite page) Craig Venter re-outfitted his yacht, the *Sorcerer II*, as a laboratory ship and sent it on a journey to sample the water of the world's oceans in the mid-2000s. Scientists on the ship filtered the water to remove microorganisms and sent the filters back to Venter's institute, which mass-sequenced the microbes' genomes. The *Sorcerer II* left Halifax, Nova Scotia, Canada, in August 2003, followed the path shown here, and returned about two years later.

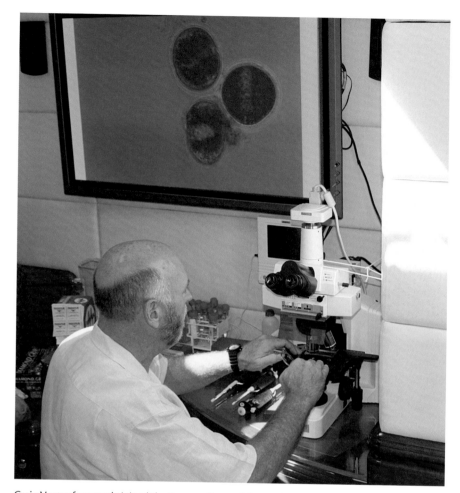

Craig Venter frequently joined the *Sorcerer II* expedition on its round-the-world travels. He is shown here on board the ship, looking through a microscope at some of the microorganisms whose genomes he plans to sequence. (*J. Craig Venter Institute*)

particularly in the United States, had become greatly concerned about possible terrorist activity, including bioterrorist attacks using natural or genetically engineered microbes. Scientists and government representatives therefore debated whether research findings that showed potential for terrorist exploitation should be published.

After some discussion, the National Science Advisory Board for Biosecurity, a government committee established to review such research, gave Venter permission to publish his group's virus paper. The paper appeared in the *Proceedings of the National Academy of Sciences* on December 23, 2003.

At a press conference held when the journal was published, Secretary of Energy Spencer Abraham (1952–   ) called the Venter team's achievement "nothing short of amazing."

SYNTHETIC BIOLOGY: ENGINEERING LIFE

Craig Venter's attempt to synthesize a minimal bacterium is one of many experiments going on in the new scientific field of *synthetic biology*. Synthetic biologists aim to turn what they see as the relatively crude alterations involved in past genetic engineering into true engineering: assembling biological circuits and perhaps even whole organisms to exact specifications from standardized parts, just as traditional engineers combine electronic switches and circuits to make television sets or computers. The components that synthetic biologists plan to use are stretches of DNA comprising sets of genes (often from different species) that make cells perform particular functions. Synthetic biology pioneer Tom Knight calls these "BioBricks."

"The goal of synthetic biology is to turn biotechnology into industrialized biotechnology," says Jay Keasling of the University of California, Berkeley, another groundbreaking synthetic biology researcher. Keasling has modified yeast and *E. coli* bacteria to make them produce artemisinin, a drug able to destroy the microorganism that causes malaria. (Malaria, a serious blood disease, kills a million people a year, mostly in developing countries in the tropics.) Artemisinin comes from a Chinese plant, but synthesizing it could make it available more cheaply. Other biotechnology companies, including Craig Venter's Synthetic Genomics, hope to use synthetic biology to make inexpensive, nonpolluting biofuels.

Some organizations, including the ETC Group, have voiced fears that microorganisms created by synthetic biologists will escape into the environment and create untold damage or that bioterrorists will release such organisms to start epidemics. These fears are similar to those expressed in the mid-1970s, when the public first became aware of genetic engineering. Like the early genetic engineers, synthetic biologists hope to deflect criticism by policing themselves, for instance by having companies that sell gene components screen orders to make sure that no one is asking for parts that could be combined to create a disease-causing microbe.

After synthesizing the phi-X174 virus, Smith, Hutchinson, and their coworkers returned to experimenting on *Mycoplasma genitalium*. They began by repeating and refining the experiments aimed at determining the minimal genome that they had performed in the late 1990s. In January 2006, they stated that only 382 of *M. genitalium*'s 482 genes appear to be necessary for life. They said that they would try to synthesize this minimal genome, creating a completely artificial living thing.

MID-DECADE CHANGES

Both Craig Venter and his yacht sailed into rough waters in 2004. Venter's marriage to Claire Fraser had been troubled for some time because of disagreements about the management of TIGR and other subjects, and they separated in that year. They divorced in February 2005, and Fraser married geneticist Stephen B. Liggett a few months later. Venter, for his part, became

French government officials temporarily halted the *Sorcerer II* in French Polynesia while they debated whether to allow the ship's scientists to take samples from French territorial waters. The *Sorcerer II* is shown here at anchor in the Marquesas Islands. *(J. Craig Venter Institute)*

The design of the J. Craig Venter Institute building in Rockville, Maryland, shown here in 2007, is supposed to resemble the color-coded pattern that reveals the sequence of bases in DNA. Venter combined several of his previous research institutions to form the institute in 2006. *(David S Holloway/Getty Images)*

engaged in July 2006 to Heather Kowalski, who had been his publicist at Celera and followed him to his new institutes.

While Venter's marriage was breaking up at home, the *Sorcerer II* expedition was forced to a temporary halt in French Polynesia. The ETC Group had continued its protests, saying that the Venter scientists were violating United Nations rules about respecting nations' biological heritage, and this time the French government shared the group's concerns. The French Ministry of Foreign Affairs denied the team a permit to conduct research in Polynesian waters and held up the expedition for three weeks. Venter enlisted French scientists to lobby the government on his behalf, however, and they eventually persuaded officials to let the sampling proceed. The expedition then continued until the end of 2005.

The *Sorcerer II* research team published three papers about their findings in *PloS Biology* in spring 2007, revealing that they had discovered 6 million new genes and 400 new species of microorganisms. Among other things, they found that all the organisms contain proteins that can detect colored light. The microbes do not use the light to make food, as plants do through the process of photosynthesis, but instead store its energy, becoming living solar batteries. In an interview published in the Summer 2006 issue of *OnEarth,* Venter said that each sample of water had a unique assortment of bacteria and viruses. He saw the ecosystem represented by such a sample as "equivalent to [a] complex multicellular organism," a "loosely associated megaspecies" in which different types of microbes specialize to carry out different functions, just as different kinds of cells do in the body of a plant or animal.

Venter reorganized his research institutions as well as his personal life in the mid-2000s. In October 2004, he consolidated his three previous institutes into a single organization, the J. Craig Venter Institute; TIGR became part of the institute two years later. (Claire Fraser left TIGR in April 2007.) Venter wrote in *A Life Decoded* that his new institute was "one of the largest private research institutes in the world," with more than 500 employees, 250,000 square feet (23,226 sq m) of laboratory space, and $200 million in assets.

ENERGY FROM ALGAE

Craig Venter and Hamilton Smith also founded a for-profit company called Synthetic Genomics on June 29, 2005, to handle the commercial applications of the synthetic microorganisms that the two hoped to produce. The company was originally located in Rockville, Maryland, near Venter's other organizations, but it soon moved to La Jolla, California. Venter hired his old friend Ari Patrinos to be the president of the new business in February 2006; Venter himself was its CEO.

In July 2009, ExxonMobil announced that it would carry out a program to develop biofuels from *algae* in collaboration with Synthetic Genomics. Synthetic Genomics had already engineered algae to secrete substances similar to intermediate products in a refinery, and the new project planned to test thousands of strains of algae to find the most efficient and economical ones for fuel production. The giant oil company promised to invest more than $600 million in the venture, divided equally between Venter's company and a research team within ExxonMobil itself. According to an Earth2tech.com online news article issued at the time of the announcement, ExxonMobil expected the Synthetic Genomics group to focus primarily on microengineering, whereas the ExxonMobil team would concentrate on scaling up processes for commercialization.

Algae have several advantages over other sources of biofuels. For one thing, the plants do not need to take up valuable farmland because they are so tiny. Since algae use carbon dioxide as a starting material to produce energy, they might also help to lower the amount of this greenhouse gas in the atmosphere and thus reduce global warming. They are more efficient at releasing energy than other sources of biofuel, such as ethanol from corn, and the fuel they make is less polluting. Growing them in commercial quantities is presently expensive, however, and genetically altered algae might prove harmful if they escaped into the environment. The scientists at Synthetic Genomics and ExxonMobil know they will have many problems to solve before making fuel from algae becomes practical.

AMBITIOUS PROGRAMS

Craig Venter launched other ambitious research programs in the late 2000s. One was the Air Genome Project, which proposed to shotgun-sequence microbes captured from the air of cities in much the same way that the Venter Institute scientists were doing with microorganisms in the world's oceans. The project's first sampling station, set up in April 2005, was on top of a 40-story office tower in downtown New York City. "With information [from this project] . . . I can not only study new ways to monitor air quality and monitor bioterrorism but also see if there is a way to harness these organisms and their clever chemistry in cleanups," Venter wrote in his autobiography.

Venter launched a second *Sorcerer* expedition in March 2009, focusing on the Baltic, Black, and Mediterranean Seas. "The[se] seas are of scientific interest because they are among the world's largest and most isolated from major oceans, and likely the source of unique marine microbial communities," Venter said in an article in the *San Diego Business Journal*.

The Venter Institute and Synthetic Genomics also formed a new company called Synthetic Genomics Vaccines Inc. to apply synthetic genomic techniques to the making of vaccines, an approach called *reverse vaccinology*. In October 2010, this company announced a three-year partnership with drug giant Novartis, supported by an award from the U.S. Biomedical Advanced Research and Development Authority, to perfect a faster process for making flu vaccines.

Building on sequencing of flu virus genes taking place at the institute, the new Venter company and Novartis plan to develop a bank of synthetically constructed *seed viruses* that match different virus strains. Once the World Health Organization (WHO) has identified the strains of natural

President Barack Obama awarded Craig Venter the National Medal of Science, the highest honor that the U.S. government can give a civilian scientist, on October 7, 2009. Francis Collins also received the award. *(Ryan K. Morris/National Science and Technology Medals Foundation)*

viruses that are most active in a given year, Novartis can select the matching seeds from the bank and begin using them to produce the stock of viruses necessary to make new vaccines. This could make vaccines available up to two months sooner than would be possible with existing technology, which requires vaccine makers to grow stocks of natural viruses distributed by WHO. More rapid vaccine production could save many lives if a serious flu epidemic occurs.

The new century has also brought changes to Craig Venter's personal life. Venter joined the faculty of Harvard University in 2009, taking the first academic position he has held since he left the State University of New York in 1983. He also continued to win major awards, most notably the National Medal of Science, which President Barack Obama (1961–   ) presented to him and Francis Collins on October 7, 2009. According to a press release issued by the Venter Institute, the award recognized Venter "for his dedication to the advancement of the science of genomics, his contributions to the understanding of its implications for society, and his commitment to the clear communication of information to the scientific community, the public, and policymakers."

ARTIFICIAL LIFE?

The most exciting of Craig Venter's recent ventures is surely the continuation of his attempts to create artificial life. Venter applied for a patent on a proposed synthetic microorganism, which he called *Mycoplasma laboratorium,* in November 2006. (Some members of the press nicknamed it "Synthia.") Venter Institute researchers announced in the same month that they had transplanted the complete natural genome of one *Mycoplasma* species into the cell of another species. The transplanted genome contained a gene that made that species of microbe resistant to a certain type of antibiotic, but the recipient species lacked this gene. After the transplant, the recipient cells were able to grow in culture dishes containing the antibiotic, which showed that the genome was functioning in its new home. Essentially, the scientists said, they had converted the second species of *Mycoplasma* into the first.

In the next step toward a truly artificial microbe, Hamilton Smith's research group published a paper in *Science* in January 2008 stating that they had built a synthetic chromosome containing all the *Mycoplasma genitalium* genes that appear to be necessary for life. The group assembled the synthetic chromosome from 101 *cassettes,* or modules of genes that work together, which they obtained from commercial suppliers. Each cassette contained four or five genes and was about 6,000 base pairs long. By the end of 2008, using biochemical machinery from yeast cells to perform the assembly, the Smith group had simplified the process of making the chromosome so greatly that they could carry it out in a single step.

Scientists from the Venter Institute have continued to build on this work. Daniel Gibson and other institute researchers announced in an article, published online by *Science* on May 20, 2010, and in the printed magazine on July 2, that they had created a complete artificial genome based on the genome of *Mycoplasma mycoides,* a bacterium related to *Mycoplasma genitalium*, which they had used in some of their earlier experiments. The genome, combined from smaller stretches of synthetic DNA during three rounds of assembly in yeast, contained 1,077,947 base pairs, adding up to about 1,000 genes. The scientists then inserted the artificial genome into bacteria of another mycoplasma species, *Mycoplasma capricolum,* whose own genomes had been removed.

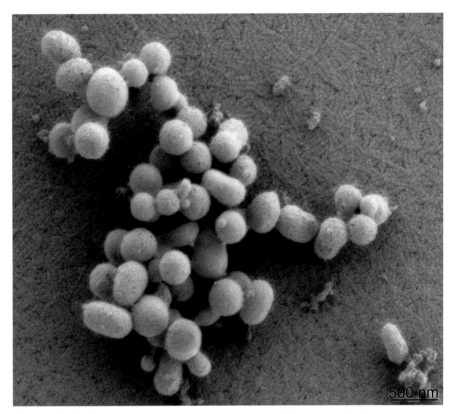

This scanning electron micrograph shows a bacterium that Craig Venter calls *Mycoplasma mycoides* JCVI-syn1. The bacterium's genome is completely artificial, assembled from genetic subunits by Venter's scientific team, yet it is able to reproduce normally and make the proteins specified by the 1,000 genes it contains. The team described the creation of the bacterium, which they say brings them significantly closer to the production of synthetic life, in May 2010. *(J. Craig Venter Institute, provided by Tom Deerinck and Mark Ellisman of the National Center for Microscopy and Imaging Research at the University of California at San Diego)*

Following this transplant, the researchers said, the microorganisms reproduced normally and made only the proteins specified by the new genes. In short, the scientists had transformed cells of *Mycoplasma capricolum* into cells of *Mycoplasma mycoides,* somewhat as they had done with natural genomes in 2006, but this time using an entirely synthetic genome. "This . . . show[ed] that we could take the [genetic] sequence out of a computer, build it and boot it up to make a synthetic cell," Gibson said.

The Venter group's achievement won an Edison Award in April 2011, and the Massachusetts Institute of Technology's *Technical Review* called it one of 10 technologies "set to transform the world." Critics insist that the Venter Institute scientists have not really created synthetic life, however. The artificial genome was essentially the same as one that already exists in nature, they point out, and it functioned only when transplanted into a natural cell.

Before he ends his scientific career, Craig Venter and his team may yet produce true synthetic life. Venter is nearing what most people would regard as retirement age, but his energy and enthusiasm seem as boundless as ever. As he told David Ewing Duncan in 2004, "All of the interesting things are still to come."

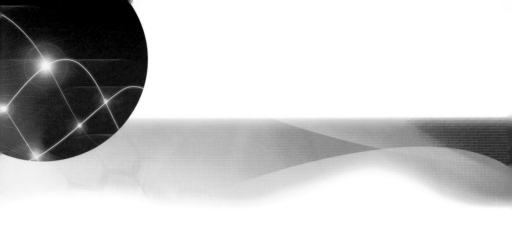

Conclusion

"The goal that I have is to make genomics transform medicine," Craig Venter told an interviewer from *BioITWorld* in November 2002. That transformation is now well underway.

PERSONALIZED MEDICINE

The sequencing of the human genome has begun to bring about the practice of *personalized medicine,* in which doctors prescribe medications and other treatments based on information about individual patients' genes rather than having a standardized treatment for everyone with a certain disease or medical condition. President Barack Obama has defined personalized medicine as "the right treatment for the right person at the right time."

Researchers have learned that variations in certain genes have major effects on the actions of drugs within the body. For instance, enzymes in the liver break down many drugs. Some people inherit forms of these enzymes that destroy the compounds more quickly than usual, so the medicines do not have a chance to take effect. Others have enzymes that break down the drugs too slowly, so they build up in the body and cause harmful *side effects.* If doctors know that patients have a gene variation that will make a particular drug ineffective, they can look for other medications that may work better. If patients have a variation that is likely to let a drug build up, the doctors can prescribe a lower dose.

Several drug companies already market some of their products along with genetic tests that can determine the medicine's effectiveness in advance. Other firms sell standalone tests that predict whether particular types of medications, such as different kinds of drugs used to treat cancer, will work in individual patients. Still other genetic tests can judge the usefulness of a whole class of treatments. For instance, after surgery to remove their tumors, some women with early stage breast cancer take a test called Oncotype-DX, which examines key genes in their tumor tissue that may have mutated as the cancer developed. This test both predicts how likely the cancer is to return and tells whether the women will benefit from chemotherapy (drug treatment). It has saved some women from having to undergo unnecessary chemotherapy treatments, which often have unpleasant and even dangerous side effects, and it has made others more willing to consider chemotherapy because it tells them that the treatments will reduce their risk of tumor recurrence substantially.

Personalized medicine is still in its infancy, but it was estimated to be a $232 billion industry in the United States in 2010, according to an article in *Modern Healthcare*. It was projected to grow by 11 percent per year. Potentially, personalized medicine can not only make drug treatment safer and more effective but can also lower health care costs by keeping patients and insurers from spending money on drugs that do not work in or are harmful to particular individuals.

GENETIC TESTS

In the years since Celera and the Human Genome Project sequenced the human genome, scientists and biotechnology companies have developed numerous genetic tests that attempt to predict illness before it happens. (An article in the Spring 2011 *Benefits Law Journal* stated that in 2010, genetic tests were available for almost 1,700 diseases.) Some of these tests can be obtained only from doctors, but consumers can order others through the mail from companies such as 23andme, Navigenics, and deCODEme. These companies ask people to send them a DNA sample in the form of saliva or a swab from the inside of their cheeks and then, for a fee ranging from several hundred to about a thousand dollars, scan the sample for gene variations associated with common illnesses. They post the results on a secure Web site, which also contains information that helps people understand the significance of their results.

Some tests identify genes that cause or are strongly associated with particular diseases. Knowing whether they carry such genes can help people make decisions such as whether (or whom) to marry or have children. Most genetic tests on the market today, however, identify gene variations associated only with increased risk of developing certain illnesses, such as heart disease, cancer, or diabetes. Some of these tests can help people make wise lifestyle choices; for instance, if people know they have a relatively high risk of developing heart disease or diabetes, they might try to reduce that risk by eating a diet low in fat or sugar and by exercising often. Researchers have warned, however, that the scientific evidence supporting many of these genetic links is weak. In any case, they stress, genes tell only part of the story: factors in the environment can play at least as great a role in determining whether a person will be sick or healthy.

Today's genetic tests scan only a small number of key genes. In another decade or so, however, many people may have the comprehensive knowledge about themselves that today only Craig Venter and a handful of other people possess: the complete sequence of their individual genomes. Thanks to advances in sequencing technology, the cost of sequencing a complete human genome has fallen drastically, to around $20,000, and some scientists think it will soon reach $1000 or less. Some have predicted that by 2020, all babies will have their genomes automatically scanned at birth, and a genome sequence will be a permanent part of everyone's medical records.

OTHER ADVANCES

Knowledge of the human genome and the way genes vary in health and disease is helping researchers develop new drugs that target particular genes or genetic pathways. Herceptin, which is given to women with breast cancer who have an abnormal form of a gene called HER2, is one example. Drugs with such precise targets are less likely to cause side effects than more broadspectrum drugs because they probably will not damage healthy cells. Knowing the sequence of the genomes of microbes, such as those that Venter's scientific teams produced, can help drug company scientists design new antibiotics.

Advances growing out of genomics are not limited to medicine. Mass sequencing of the genomes of organisms in particular ecosystems, which Craig Venter helped to pioneer with his ocean studies, can reveal how organisms relate to one another, how they evolved, and how environmental changes affect them. Knowledge of the genomes of single-celled organisms not only helps scientists understand the vital role of these organisms in the world's ecologies but can lead to their modification to solve environmental problems and serve other human uses, as Venter's Synthetic Genomics is attempting to do in making biofuels from algae. Knowledge of plant genomes can help agricultural researchers develop food crops that resist drought, insects, and disease.

When Craig Venter returned from Vietnam, he vowed that his life would make a difference to the world. Researchers are just beginning to explore the new genomic frontiers opened up by the techniques that Venter helped to pioneer. Already, though, it seems obvious that he has achieved his goal.

Chronology

1910
Thomas Hunt Morgan uses fruit flies to show that an inherited characteristic is associated with a particular chromosome

October 14, 1946
John Craig Venter is born in Salt Lake City, Utah

April 1953
James Watson and Francis Crick work out the structure of the DNA molecule and show how the molecule reproduces

August 25, 1967
Venter begins service as a navy hospital corpsman in Vietnam

August 29, 1968
Venter's military service ends

November 1968
Venter marries Barbara Rae

1969
Venter studies at the College of San Mateo

1970
Venter transfers to the University of California, San Diego

1971
With Nathan Kaplan, Venter does experiments to show that adrenalin enters cells by binding to receptors

1972
Venter publishes first scientific paper

June 1972
Venter earns B.S. in biochemistry from University of California, San Diego

1973
Two California scientists invent genetic engineering

1975
Frederick Sanger develops technique for determining the sequence of bases in a short stretch of DNA

December 1975
Venter earns Ph.D. in physiology and pharmacology from University of California, San Diego

1976
Carl Woese proposes that certain microorganisms belong to an evolutionary third kingdom, the archaea

July 1976
Venter joins faculty of State University of New York, Buffalo

March 8, 1977
Venter's son, Christopher, born

1980
Congress passes Bayh-Dole Act; U.S. Supreme Court rules that living things can be patented if humans have altered them

1981
Venter and Barbara divorce; Venter marries Claire Fraser; moves to biochemistry department

1982
Venter becomes full professor and deputy director of molecular immunology department at Roswell Park Cancer Center

1984
Venter and Fraser join National Institutes of Health (NIH)

1985
Scientists begin to consider sequencing the human genome

1986
Venter's laboratory isolates adrenalin receptor gene from human brain; Venter learns about automated sequencing machines; Charles DeLisi and James Watson take steps to initiate a human genome sequencing project

1987
Venter's team works out the sequence of the brain adrenalin receptor gene; Congress authorizes first payment for a program to sequence the human genome, and James Watson and other scientists begin planning the project

February 1987
Venter receives first automated DNA sequencing machine

fall 1987
Venter publishes first papers using data with an automated sequencer

1988
Venter stops work on receptors and begins involvement with human genome sequencing project

October 1988
Congress gives Human Genome Project its name and places James Watson in charge of it

1990
Venter and Mark Adams begin shotgun sequencing complementary DNA libraries from brain cells; using expressed sequence tags (ESTs), they discover hundreds of new genes; Human Genome Project officially begins

June 20, 1991
NIH files patent application on 337 ESTs discovered by Venter's laboratory

June 21, 1991
Venter and Adams publish paper on using ESTs to discover brain genes in *Science*

July 1991
Watson criticizes Venter's sequencing technique and the patenting of ESTs

early 1992
NIH applies for patent on 2,375 more ESTs; biotechnology companies try to hire Venter

April 10, 1992
Watson resigns as head of Human Genome Project

June 10, 1992
Venter and Wallace Steinberg agree to establish The Institute for Genomic Research (TIGR), a nonprofit institute to be headed by Venter, which will be linked to a for-profit company, Human Genome Sciences

January 1993
TIGR and Human Genome Sciences become operational; TIGR begins Human Gene Anatomy Project

early 1993
Francis Collins becomes director of the Human Genome Project; Venter becomes friends with Hamilton Smith

May 1993
Pharmaceutical giant SmithKline Beecham signs contract with Human Genome Sciences for exclusive right to create drugs from TIGR's discoveries

September 1993
Hamilton Smith suggests that TIGR sequence the genome of the bacterium *Hemophilus influenzae*

late 1993
Venter uses TIGR EST database to help Bert Vogelstein locate a gene that causes some cases of colon cancer

1994
Venter develops a stress-related colon inflammation and has to have surgery

February 1994
Smith prepares a library of DNA segments from *Hemophilus influenzae*

April 1995
TIGR team finishes sequencing the *Hemophilus influenzae* genome; Claire Fraser's group sequences genome of another bacterium, *Mycoplasma genitalium*

May 24, 1995
Venter and Smith announce the sequencing of the first complete genome of a living thing *(H. influenzae)*

July 28, 1995
Venter group's paper on the *H. influenzae* sequence appears in *Science*

September 1995
Nature publishes most of the ESTs from Human Gene Anatomy Project

October 20, 1995
Fraser's group publishes paper on *Mycoplasma genitalium* genome sequence in *Science*

late 1995
Scott Peterson and Clyde Hutchinson determine the minimum collection of genes necessary to keep *M. genitalium* alive

1996
TIGR sequences genomes of bacteria that cause several kinds of disease

August 1996
Venter's group publishes genome sequence of *Methanococcus jannaschii,* a member of the archaea

June 20, 1997
Venter separates TIGR from Human Genome Sciences and posts large amounts of TIGR's genome data on the Internet

November 1997
Executives at Applied Biosystems and parent company Perkin-Elmer Corporation begin considering sequencing the human genome

February 1998
Venter and Mark Adams see prototype of new sequencing machines at Applied Biosystems; Venter agrees to lead the proposed human genome sequencing project; prepares business plan for new company he will head

May 8, 1998
Perkin-Elmer executives approve human genome sequencing project and Venter's new company; Venter tells Harold Varmus and Francis Collins about the project

May 10, 1998
A *New York Times* article announces that Venter's private company has promised to sequence the human genome faster and more cheaply than the Human Genome Project

May 13, 1998
HGP scientists greet Venter with hostility at Cold Spring Harbor meeting; Gerald Rubin agrees to let Venter's company sequence the fruit fly genome

August 1998
Venter opens Celera Genomics

October 1998
Human Genome Project scientists announce their plan to produce a rough draft of the human genome sequence by the end of 2000

December 1998
First automatic sequencing machines arrive at Celera

1999
Panel of ethicists and religious leaders convened by Venter concludes that Venter's plan to make an artificial microorganism is not morally wrong

February 1999
Hamilton Smith prepares fruit fly DNA libraries for sequencing; HGP reduces number of sequencing centers to five

March 15, 1999
HGP moves date for finishing its rough sequence draft forward to spring 2000; Celera also moves its target date forward

April 1999
Celera scientists begin sequencing the fruit fly genome

early 1999
Three large drug companies sign up for Celera's database service

July 1999
Smith begins preparing libraries from five samples of human DNA, including samples from Venter and himself

late August 1999
Celera's first attempt to assemble the fruit fly genome fails because of an error in its computer program

September 8, 1999
Celera finishes sequencing fruit fly genome and begins on the human; the company's computer program assembles the fly genome successfully

November 1999
Celera hosts an annotation jamboree, in which fruit fly experts analyze the fly genome

February 28, 2000
HGP leaders and Wellcome Trust send a letter to Celera, stating their grievances against the company

March 5, 2000
Wellcome Trust leaks the letter to *Los Angeles Times,* which prints it

March 14, 2000
Value of biotechnology stocks, including Celera's, drops abruptly after Bill Clinton and Tony Blair make a statement that appears to disapprove of gene patenting

March 24, 2000
Venter's group publishes three papers about the fruit fly genome in *Science*

May 2000
Aristides Patrinos arranges meetings between Venter and Collins, during which they agree to make a joint announcement about finishing the rough draft of the human genome sequence

June 26, 2000
In a ceremony at the White House, Venter and Collins, accompanied by President Clinton, announce completion of the human genome sequence

2001
Executives of Applera, Celera's parent company, change Celera's focus to proteins and drug development

February 15, 2001
Nature publishes HGP paper about the human genome sequence

February 16, 2001
Science publishes Celera's paper about the human genome sequence

April 27, 2001
Celera publishes paper announcing the sequencing of the mouse genome

2001–2002
Venter receives major international science awards and is elected to the U.S. National Academy of Sciences

January 21, 2002
Applera executives fire Venter as head of Celera

late April 2002
Venter establishes three new research institutes that he will head

November 2002
Department of Energy (DOE) gives Venter's Institute for Biological Energy Alternatives (IBEA) $3 million to begin developing synthetic microorganisms that can help the environment

spring 2003
DOE gives IBEA another $9 million for the synthetic microbe project

February and May 2003
Researchers from IBEA collect samples of water from the Sargasso Sea; Venter's team mass-sequences the genomes of microorganisms in the water

April 2003
Human Genome Project announces finished sequence of the human genome

August 2003
Sorcerer II expedition begins

November 2003
Venter Institute scientists announce that they have synthesized a virus, phi-X174

April 2, 2004
Venter's group publishes results of Sargasso Sea expedition in *Science*

October 2004
Venter consolidates his three institutes to form the J. Craig Venter Institute

February 2005
Venter and Fraser divorce

June 28, 2005
Venter and Hamilton Smith form Synthetic Genomics, a for-profit company that will handle commercial applications of the synthetic microorganisms that the group hopes to create

2006
TIGR becomes part of the Venter Institute

January 2006
Venter researchers announce that only 382 of *Mycoplasma genitalium*'s genes are necessary for life and say they plan to use this minimal genome as the basis for an artificial microorganism

July 2006
Venter becomes engaged to Heather Kowalski

November 2006
Venter applies for patent on his proposed synthetic microorganism; Venter Institute scientists announce that they have changed one species of *Mycoplasma* into another by transplanting a whole natural genome from one species to the other

spring 2007
Sorcerer II expedition team publishes papers about its findings

2008
Genetic Information Nondiscrimination Act (GINA) becomes law

February 2008
Hamilton Smith and others publish paper saying that they have built an artificial chromosome containing all the genes needed for *Mycoplasma*

late 2008
Smith group says they can now make the artificial chromosome in a single step

2009
Venter joins faculty of Harvard University

March 2009
Venter launches second *Sorcerer II* expedition

July 2009
ExxonMobil announces that it and Synthetic Genomics will collaborate on a project to develop biofuels from algae

October 7, 2009
Venter and Francis Collins receive National Medal of Science

May 2010
Venter Institute scientists announce that they have built a completely synthetic genome, based on the natural genome of a bacterial species, and inserted it into bacteria of a related species from which the original genomes had been removed, creating healthy bacteria that showed all the characteristics of the species represented by the synthetic genome

October 2010
Venter forms a new company, Synthetic Genomics Vaccines Inc., that will work with the Swiss drug firm Novartis to create a library of synthetic seed viruses of various influenza strains, thereby increasing the speed with which new flu vaccines can be made

April 2011
Venter group's creation of a bacterium with an artifical genome wins Edison Award; MIT's *Technology Review* calls it one of 10 technologies "set to transform the world"

Glossary

adenine (A)   one of the four bases in DNA; it always pairs with thymine.

adrenalin   a hormone produced by the adrenal glands, which governs the fight-or-flight reaction.

algae   a group of plantlike, water-dwelling organisms, many of which have only a single cell

amino acid   one of 20 types of small molecules of which proteins are made. *See also* PROTEIN.

annotation   the process of analyzing a genome to determine the functions of its genes, similarities with genes of other organisms, and so on.

archaea   a group of microorganisms that make up a third branch in the evolutionary tree of life, comparable to prokaryotes and eukaryotes. *See also* EUKARYOTE; PROKARYOTE.

bacterial artificial chromosome (BAC) clone   one of the large segments of DNA into which the Human Genome Project divided the genomes it sequenced.

bases   the four smaller molecules (adenine, cytosine, guanine, and thymine) that, arranged in pairs, make up the part of the DNA molecule that carries the genetic code.

biotechnology   the technology of using other organisms, especially genetically altered microorganisms, for the benefit of humans.

cassette   a group of genes that work together, sold as a module.

chromosome   one of a group of paired, wormlike structures in the cell nucleus of eukaryotic organisms, made up of protein and DNA.

clone   an exact genetic duplicate.

complementary   able to work with another part to complete a whole; in DNA, the base adenine (A) is complementary to (always pairs with) the base thymine (T), and guanine (G) is complementary to cytosine (C). The two strands of the DNA molecule are also complementary to each other.

complementary DNA (cDNA)   a single strand of DNA whose base sequence is complementary to a strand of messenger RNA; it contains only expressed genetic material. *See also* COMPLEMENTARY; EXPRESSED; MESSENGER RNA.

contig   (short for "contiguous segment") a segment of DNA ending in a sequence that is complementary to (overlaps) the beginning sequence of another segment. *See also* SCAFFOLD; UNITIG.

culture   a colony of cells or microorganisms raised in a laboratory container.

cytoplasm   the jellylike substance in the main body of cells.

cytosine (C)   one of the four bases in DNA; it always pairs with guanine.

deoxyribonucleic acid (DNA)   the biochemical that carries inherited information in most organisms; each DNA molecule consists of a pair of long, intertwined strands of smaller molecules.

DNA polymerase   an enzyme that can assemble a complementary strand of DNA onto a single-stranded DNA template from free-floating nucleotides.

dominant trait   a characteristic that shows itself in an organism if the organism inherits the gene for that trait from either parent. *Compare* RECESSIVE TRAIT.

environmental genomics (metagenomics)   the study of all the genomes in an ecosystem, or a sample of an ecosystem, as a unit.

enzyme   one of a class of proteins that speeds up, or makes possible, chemical reactions in a cell.

Escherichia coli (E. coli)   a bacterium that lives, usually harmlessly, in the human intestine; it is frequently used in genetic experiments.

eukaryote   an organism whose cells have a nucleus; one of the three main branches (kingdoms) in the evolutionary tree of life. *See also* ARCHAEA; NUCLEUS; PROKARYOTE.

expressed   used to make proteins in a cell.

expressed sequence tag (EST)   a short stretch of single-stranded DNA that can be used to locate a gene containing a complementary sequence.

fruit fly   a small insect *(Drosophila melanogaster)* often used in genetic experiments.

GenBank   a public (free-access) international database of genes and DNA sequences.

gene   a segment of DNA containing the code for making one protein or carrying out another single task in a cell.

genetic engineering   the technology of artificially altering genes or genomes, especially by inserting DNA from one organism or species into the genome of another.

Genetic Information Nondiscrimination Act (GINA)   a federal law passed in 2008 that forbids employers or health insurers to discriminate against people on the basis of genetic information.

genetics   the study of biological inheritance in terms of individual genes. *Compare* GENOMICS.

genome   an organism's complete collection of genetic material.

genomics   the study of genomes as whole units. *Compare* GENETICS.

guanine (G)   one of the four bases in DNA; it always pairs with cytosine.

Hemophilus influenzae   a microorganism that can cause ear, lung, and brain infections in children; its genome was the first genome of a living thing to be sequenced.

hormone   a biochemical produced in one part of the body that affects cells in another part of the body.

Human Genome Project (HGP)   an international project to work out the complete sequence of bases in the human genome; the project, which was sponsored chiefly by the U.S. government, existed from 1990 to 2003.

informed consent   the act of formally consenting to a medical treatment or test after having been told of all possible risks and side effects.

junk DNA   old term for stretches of DNA with no known function that lie between, and sometimes within, genes; scientists now believe that these stretches do have functions, though they are not sure what they are.

library   a group of short DNA segments from a particular cell type or genome, each of which is grown in a separate colony of cloned bacteria.

messenger RNA   a short-lived form of single-stranded RNA, complementary to a segment of DNA (gene) in the cell nucleus that carries the code for making a protein; the messenger RNA transmits the code from the nucleus to the cytoplasm of the cell, where the protein will be made. *See also* RIBONUCLEIC ACID.

metagenomics   *See* ENVIRONMENTAL GENOMICS.

Methanococcus jannaschii   an oceanic microorganism belonging to the archaea; it was the first member of the archaea to have its genome sequenced. *See also* ARCHAEA.

mutation   a change in a gene.

Mycoplasma genitalium   a small bacterium that lives in the human genital tract; scientists have studied its genome to determine the minimum set of genes necessary to sustain life.

nucleotide   a unit of which DNA is composed, consisting of a base attached to a molecule of sugar and a molecule of phosphate. *See also* BASES.

nucleus   the central body of a cell, containing the chromosomes and DNA that carry inherited information. *See also* CHROMOSOME; *compare* CYTOPLASM.

oligonucleotide   a short stretch of DNA, made up of multiple nucleotides. *See also* NUCLEOTIDE.

patent   an agreement between an inventor and a government, in which the government grants exclusive rights to profit from an invention for a limited time period in exchange for the inventor's publishing the details of the invention.

personalized medicine   the practice of choosing medical treatments based on an individual's genetic information.

plasmid   a small, ring-shaped piece of DNA, often used to transfer foreign genes into bacteria.

preexisting condition   a medical condition from which a person suffered before applying for health or life insurance; an insurance company can refuse to insure someone or charge the person higher premiums if the person has a preexisting condition.

prokaryote   an organism, usually a microorganism, whose cells do not have nuclei; prokaryotes are one of the three main branches (kingdoms) of the evolutionary tree of life. *See also* ARCHAEA; EUKARYOTE.

protein   one of a large class of biochemicals that does most of the work in cells.

receptor   a protein molecule on the surface of a cell that interacts with only one or a small number of other proteins; when a protein such as a hormone binds to its receptor, the combined molecule moves into the cell and causes changes there.

recessive trait   a characteristic that is visible in an organism only when the organism inherits genes for that characteristic from both parents. *Compare* DOMINANT TRAIT.

reverse vaccinology   the technology of using genomics to design vaccines.

ribonucleic acid (RNA)   a biochemical similar to DNA except that it contains one different type of base (uracil instead of thymine); it translates the code carried in DNA into a form that can be used to make proteins. *See also* DEOXYRIBONUCLEIC ACID (DNA).

scaffold   a long stretch of DNA made up of many overlapping contigs or unitigs. *See also* CONTIG; UNITIG.

seed virus   the starter culture from which large stocks of virus are made for vaccine production.

sequencing   the act of determining the order, or sequence, of bases in all or part of a DNA molecule.

shotgun sequencing   the process of dividing a long DNA segment into many small parts, sequencing all or a portion of each part, and using computers to reassemble the sequences in the correct order. *See also* WHOLE-GENOME SHOTGUN SEQUENCING.

side effects   unwanted effects of a medical treatment.

single-nucleotide polymorphisms (SNPs)   segments of DNA that exist in several variations in different members of a species; the segments differ by only a single base.

synthetic biology   the new science of making biological circuits or possibly even whole organisms from standardized genetic parts.

thymine (T)   one of the four kinds of bases in DNA; it always pairs with adenine.

unitig   unique continuous fragments, segments of DNA whose ending sequence matches the beginning sequence of only one other segment in the genome. *See also* CONTIG; SCAFFOLD.

whole-genome shotgun sequencing   the process of applying shotgun sequencing to a whole genome at once. *See also* SHOTGUN SEQUENCING.

X chromosome   a chromosome that helps to determine gender in many organisms; females inherit an X chromosome from both parents, whereas males inherit an X chromosome from their mothers and a different chromosome, the Y chromosome, from their fathers.

Further Resources

Books
Ashburner, M. *Won for All: How the* Drosophila *Genome Was Sequenced.* Cold Spring Harbor, N.Y.: Cold Spring Harbor Press, 2006.

A short, candid account of the sequencing of the fruit fly genome (in which Craig Venter played a major part), written by one of the participants.

Collins, Francis. *The Language of Life.* New York: HarperCollins, 2010.

Collins, former head of the Human Genome Project, describes the improvements in medicine that have grown out of the project, including the use of individuals' genetic information to tailor medical treatments to their specific needs.

Cook-Deegan, Robert. *The Gene Wars: Science, Politics, and the Human Genome.* New York: W. W. Norton, 1994.

Provides background on the early history of the Human Genome Project, before Craig Venter's involvement.

Davies, Kevin. *Cracking the Genome: Inside the Race to Unlock Human DNA.* New York: Free Press, 2001.

One of several books describing the "race" between Craig Venter's company, Celera Genomics, and the Human Genome Project to produce a rough draft of the complete sequence of the human genome.

Duncan, David Ewing. *The Geneticist Who Played Hoops with My DNA . . . and Other Masterminds from the Frontiers of Biotech.* New York: William Morrow, 2005.

Contains a chapter on Venter and a chapter on Francis Collins, based on interviews in the early 2000s.

Shreeve, James. *The Genome War: How Craig Venter Tried to Capture the Code of Life and Save the World.* New York: Ballantine Books, 2005.

Shreeve observed Venter and the other scientists at Celera Genomics as they sequenced the fruit fly and human genomes.

Sulston, John, and Georgina Ferry. *The Common Thread: A Story of Science, Politics, Ethics, and the Human Genome.* Washington, D.C.: Joseph Henry Press, 2001.
Story of the "human genome race" told from the point of view of the scientist who headed the part of the Human Genome Project that was done in Britain. Sulston strongly questions Venter's motives and his attitude about access to scientific information.

Venter, J. Craig. *A Life Decoded: My Genome: My Life.* New York: Viking/ Penguin, 2007.
Venter's autobiography, including descriptions of some of the gene variants in his genome and their implications for his health.

"Venter, J. Craig." *Current Biography Yearbook 1995.* Bronx, New York: H. W. Wilson, 1995, pp. 573–577.
Details Venter's background and early career, including quotations from popular articles.

Watson, James. *DNA: The Secret of Life.* New York: Alfred A. Knopf, 2003.
History of research on DNA and descriptions of some of the areas of science and society it has influenced, written by the codiscoverer of the DNA molecule's structure. It includes some material on the history of the Human Genome Project.

Wickelgren, Ingrid. *The Gene Masters: How a New Breed of Scientific Entrepreneurs Raced for the Biggest Prize in Biology.* New York: Times Books/ Henry Holt, 2002.
Another account of the competition between Craig Venter's private company and the government-sponsored Human Genome Project to sequence the human genome.

Internet Resources

Davies, Kevin, John Russell, and John Dodge. "John Craig Venter Unvarnished." *Bio-IT World.* Available online. URL: http://www.bio-itworld.com/ archive/111202/horizons_venter.html and http://www.bio-itworld.com/ archive/121002/horizons_venter.html. November and December 2002. Accessed June 5, 2011.
Long interview with Venter about his achievements and career plans, soon after he left Celera Genomics.

Gross, Liza. "Untapped Bounty: Sampling the Seas to Survey Microbial Biodiversity." Public Library of Science, *PloS Biology*. Available online. URL: http://www.ploscollections.org/article/info%3Adoi%2F10.1371%2Fjournal. pbio.0050085;jsessionid=E0442FC2B6CE56D499DBE8DB3D65D865. March 13, 2007. Accessed June 5, 2011.

Summary of the procedures and results of Venter's Sorcerer II expedition, which sampled water from the world's oceans and mass-sequenced the genomes of the microorganisms in the samples.

"J. Craig Venter Institute." J. Craig Venter Institute. Available online. URL: http://www.jcvi.org. Accessed June 5, 2011.

Web site of Venter's research institute includes history of the institute, scientific papers, and news releases about current research projects.

Levy, S., et al. "The Diploid Genome Sequence of an Individual Human." Public Library of Science, *PloS Biology*. Available online. URL: http://www. plosbiology.org/article/info:doi/10.1371/journal.pbio.0050254. September 4, 2007. Accessed June 5, 2011.

Paper describing the complete sequencing of the genome of Craig Venter, the first individual to have his genome sequenced.

Mayo Clinic staff. "Pharmacogenomics: When Medicine Gets Personal." Mayo Clinic. Available online. URL: http://www.mayoclinic.com/health/ personalized-medicine/ca00078. Last modified July 16, 2010. Accessed June 5, 2011.

Fact sheet describes personalized medicine, or pharmacogenomics, using an individual's genetic information to determine how he or she will react to drugs or other medical treatments.

Nicholls, Henry. "*Sorcerer II*: The Search for Microbial Diversity Roils the Waters." Public Library of Science, *PloS Biology*. Available online. URL: http://www.ploscollections.org/article/info%3Adoi%2F10.1371%2Fjournal. pbio.0050074;jsessionid=E0442FC2B6CE56D499DBE8DB3D65D865. March 13, 2007. Accessed June 5, 2011.

Discusses the ethical, legal, and environmental implications of Venter's project to sample microorganisms in the world's oceans and sequence their genomes.

"Novartis Announces Agreement to Develop Influenza Vaccines Using Revolutionary 'Synthetic Genomics' Technology" (October 7, 2010). Available online. URL: http://www.novartis.com/newsroom/media-releases/ en/2010/1449685.shtml. Accessed June 5, 2011.

Describes partnership between the giant Swiss drug firm and Venter's new company, Synthetic Genomics Vaccines Inc., to use synthetic genomic technology to create influenza vaccines more quickly than is currently possible.

Oak Ridge National Laboratory. "Human Genome Project Information." Human Genome Project. Available online. URL: http://www.ornl.gov/sci/ techresources/Human_Genome/home.shtml. Last modified May 31, 2011. Accessed June 5, 2011.

Government site includes a description and history of the project (1990–2003); its goals; its results; the ethical, legal, and social issues it raised; landmark scientific papers related to the project; educational resources; and news stories on current research that has grown out of the project.

Platoni, Kara. "Assembly Required." *Stanford Magazine*, July–August 2009. Available online. URL: http:www.stanfordalumni.org/news/magazine/2009/ julaug/features/biology.html. Accessed June 5, 2011.

Article describes synthetic biology, the attempts to create or modify living things from preassembled genetic parts.

"PMC: Personalized Medicine Coalition." Personalized Medicine Coalition. Available online. URL: http://www.personalizedmedicinecoalition.org. Accessed June 5, 2011.

Includes articles and other resources related to personalized medicine, the prescribing of medical treatments on the basis of individuals' genetic information, which the sequencing of the human genome helped to bring about.

"Rocking the Boat: J. Craig Venter's Microbial Collecting Expedition Under Fire in Latin America." ETC Group. Available online. URL: http://www. etcgroup.org/node/91. July 22, 2004. Accessed June 5, 2011.

Environmental protest group explains why it thinks Venter's Sorcerer II expedition violates the rights of countries by sampling the biodiversity of their waters.

Shreeve, James. "Craig Venter's Epic Voyage to Redefine the Origin of the Species." *Wired*. Available online. URL: http://www.wired.com/wired/ archive/12.08/venter_pr.html. August 2004. Accessed June 5, 2011.

Shreeve gives a first-hand account of part of Venter's Sorcerer II expedition and compares it to Charles Darwin's landmark voyage on the Beagle, which led to Darwin's ideas about evolution.

"Synthetic Genomics: The Global Challenge." Synthetic Genomics. Available online. URL: http://www.syntheticgenomics.com. Accessed June 5, 2011.

Web site of Venter's for-profit company describes its current research on genetically altering or synthesizing microbes to create sustainable fuels and other resources that will help humans and the environment.

Venter, Craig. "Bigger Faster Better." *Seed* magazine. Available online. URL: http://seedmagazine.com/stateofscience/sos_feature_venter_p1.html. November 20, 2008. Accessed June 5, 2011.

Venter summarizes his career and explains why he thinks that fear of involvement with private industry is holding science back.

"Welcome to the *Sorcerer II* Expedition, a Global Voyage of Discovery." J. Craig Venter Institute. Available online. URL: http://www.sorcerer2expedi tion.org/version1/HTML/main.htm. Last modified January 25, 2005. Accessed June 5, 2011.

This Web site provides details of the 2003–2004 expedition to sample the world's oceans and mass-sequence the genomes of the microbes in the samples. It includes information on the voyage route and sampling methods.

Periodicals

Adams, M. D., et al., "Complementary DNA Sequencing: Expressed Sequence Tags and the Human Genome Project," *Science* 252 (1991): 1,651–1,656.

This was the Venter group's first paper on the expressed sequence tags (ESTs) that they created from complementary DNA libraries made from brain tissue. Most of the genes from which the ESTs came were new to science.

———. "Initial Assessment of Human Gene Diversity and Expression Patterns Based upon 83 Million Nucleotides of cDNA Sequence." *Nature* 377 (Supplement, September 28, 1995): 3–174.

Contains numerous cDNA sequences and gene analysis from Venter's Human Gene Anatomy Project at TIGR.

———. "The Genome Sequence of *Drosophila Melanogaster*." *Science* 287 (March 24, 2000): 2,185–2,195.

The Celera group's scientific paper about the sequence of the fruit fly genome.

Beardsley, Timothy M. "Metagenomics Reveals Microbial Diversity." *BioScience* 56 (March 2006): 192–197.

Describes the new scientific field of metagenomics (environmental genomics), using Venter's Sorcerer II *expedition as an example.*

Bourzac, Katherine. "How to Remake Life." *Technology Review* 113 (September–October 2010): 108–110.

Recounts the process by which scientists at the Venter Institute created a complete artificial bacterial genome and transplanted it into a related species of bacteria from which the genomes had been removed, thereby transforming the recipient bacteria into the species represented by the artificial genome.

Bromund, Dave C. "Genetic Info Act Will Do More than Stop Discrimination." *Indianapolis Business Journal*, August 11, 2008.

Brief article describes the Genetic Information Nondiscrimination Act (GINA), a law that took effect in May 2008. It prevents employers and health insurers from discriminating against people on the basis of information about their genes.

Bult, C. J. "Complete Genome Sequence of the Methanogenic Archaeon, *Methanococcus Jannaschii*," *Science* 273 (1996): 1,058 ff.

TIGR's sequencing of the genome of this unusual undersea microorganism helped to prove that biologist Carl Woese was correct in placing it and similar microbes in a "third kingdom," different from both prokaryotes (bacteria and similar microorganisms) and eukaryotes (organisms whose cells have a nucleus, including plants and animals).

Chung, F. Z., et al. "Cloning and Sequence Analysis of the Human Brain Beta-Adrenergic Receptor: Evolutionary Relationship to Rodent and Avian Beta-Receptors and Porcine Muscarinic Receptors." *FEBS Letters* 211 (1987): 200–206.

This article describes the sequence of the adrenalin receptor gene in human brain and compares the gene to similar ones in rats, birds, and pigs.

Douthat, Ross. "The God of Small Things." *Atlantic* 299 (January–February 2007): 120–124.

Review of Venter's recent career, focusing on his attempts to create an artificial microorganism that will make nonpolluting fuel.

Fleischmann, R. D., et al. "Whole-Genome Random Sequencing and Assembly of *Haemophilus influenzae* Rd.," *Science* 269 (July 28, 1995): 496–512.

This paper announces the Venter group's sequencing of the genome of the bacterium Hemophilus influenzae, *the first living thing to have its genome sequenced.*

Fraser, Claire M., et al. "The Minimal Gene Complement of *Mycoplasma genitalium*." *Science* 270 (October 20, 1995): 397–403.

Fraser's group describes sequencing the genome of this bacterium, which had the smallest genome of any free-living organism known at the time.

Gibson, D. G., et al. "Complete Chemical Synthesis, Assembly, and Cloning of a *Mycoplasma genitalium* Genome." *Science* 319 (January 24, 2008): 1,215–1,220.

Paper describes the synthesis of the complete genome of a bacterium.

———. "Creation of a Bacterial Cell Controlled by a Chemically Synthesized Genome." *Science* 329 (July 2, 2010): 52–56.

Scientific paper describing the transplantation of a complete artificial bacterial genome into cells of a related species, thereby essentially changing the species of the cells.

Golden, Frederic, and Michael D. Lemonick. "The Race Is Over." *Time* 156 (July 3, 2000): 18 ff.

This news article focuses on the competition between Craig Venter of Celera Genomics and Francis Collins of the Human Genome Project and the behind-the-scenes maneuvering, especially the "pizza diplomacy" of Aristides Patrinos, that persuaded the two men to end their "race" in an amicable tie.

Howell, Katie. "Exxon Sinks $600M into Algae-Based Biofuels in Major Strategy Shift." *New York Times,* July 14, 2009.

Describes ExxonMobil's collaborative research program with Venter's company, Synthetic Genomics, to create biofuel from algae (plantlike water organisms).

Hutchinson, C. A., et al. "Global Transposon Mutagenesis and a Minimal *Mycoplasma* Genome." *Science* 286 (December 10, 1999): 2,165–2,169.

This paper recounts the original attempt to establish how many of Mycoplasma genitalium's genes are necessary for life. The scientist put one gene after another out of action by inserting transposons ("jumping genes") into the genes, then determined whether the microorganism could survive without each gene.

Jaroslovsky, Rich. "Self-Absorbed? It Must Be My Genes." *Business Week,* February 1, 2010, p. 79.

Brief review of the three chief companies offering genetic tests directly to consumers, including speed of response, the types of information given, and cost of the tests.

"J. Craig Venter, Ph.D., Announces Formation of Three Not-for-Profit Organizations." *PR Newswire*, April 30, 2002.

Venter says he will form three new organizations: The TIGR Center for the Advancement of Genomics, the Institute for Biological Energy Alternatives, and the J. Craig Venter Science Foundation.

Jegalian, Karin. "The Gene Factory." *Technology Review* 102 (March–April 1999): 64–69.

Explains how Craig Venter and Celera Genomics will use new automated sequencing machines to sequence the human genome.

Koshland, Daniel. "Frontiers in Biotechnology." *Science* 252 (June 21, 1991): 1,593.

Editorial praising Venter's use of expressed sequence tags to increase the speed of identifying genes.

Lander, E. S., et al. "Initial Sequencing and Analysis of the Human Genome." *Nature* 409 (February 15, 2001): 860–921.

The Human Genome Project's scientific paper about their sequencing of the human genome.

Lartigue, C., et al. "Genome Transplantation in Bacteria: Changing One Species to Another." *Science* 317 (August 3, 2007): 632–638.

Paper in which Venter Institute scientists announce that they have transformed one species of Mycoplasma *into another by transplanting the genome of the second species into the first.*

Marshall, Eliot. "A High-Stakes Gamble on Genome Sequencing." *Science* 284 (June 18, 1999): 1,906 ff.

Article describes Craig Venter's new company, Celera Genomics, and explains how it plans to sequence the human genome and handle accessibility to its data.

———. "Sharing the Glory, Not the Credit." *Science* 291 (February 16, 2001): 1,189 ff.

News article details the arguments between Craig Venter and Human Genome Project scientists about how data and publications stemming from the sequencing of the human genome should be handled and explains why Science *chose to accept Venter's terms for publication.*

Nicoliades, N. C., et al. "Mutations of Two *PMS* Homologs in Hereditary Nonpolyposis Colon Cancer." *Nature* 371 (1994): 75–80.

Paper in which Johns Hopkins University scientist Bert Vogelstein shows that two genes similar to bacterial genes that repair errors in DNA reproduction are altered in a type of inherited human colon cancer. Vogelstein located these genes by consulting the database of expressed sequence tags for human genes that Craig Venter had created at The Institute for Genomic Research.

Nowak, Rachel. "Bacterial Genome Sequence Bagged." *Science* 269 (July 28, 1995): 468–470.

News article accompanying scientific paper in which Venter and Hamilton Smith report that they have produced the first complete sequence of the genome of a living thing, the bacterium Hemophilus influenzae. *The article explains the significance of the achievement.*

Office of the Press Secretary. "Remarks by the President, Prime Minister Tony Blair of England (via Satellite), Dr. Francis Collins, Director of the National Human Genome Research Institute, and Dr. Craig Venter, President and Chief Scientific Officer, Celera Genomics Corporation, on the Completion of the First Survey of the Entire Human Genome Project." *M2 Presswire*, June 30, 2000.

Complete text of the speeches of the four men during the White House ceremony marking this historic occasion.

"Patent Pending: Artificial Life." *Economist* 383 (June 16, 2007): 94.

Announces that Greg Venter has applied for a patent on Mycoplasma laboratorium, *the synthetic microorganism he plans to create. The article also describes the objections of the ETC Group and others to Venter's research and patent application.*

Pennisi, Elizabeth. "Finally, the Book of Life and Instructions for Navigating It." *Science* 288 (June 30, 2000): 2,304 ff.

News article announcing the sequencing of a rough draft of the human genome by the Human Genome Project and Celera Genomics, including the different techniques the groups used and the next steps in understanding the human genome.

———. "The Human Genome." *Science* 291 (February 16, 2001): 1,177.

Brief article summarizes the Venter group's scientific paper about sequencing the human genome, which appears in the same issue.

———, and Eliot Marshall. "Hubris and the Human Genome." *Science* 280 (May 15, 1998): 994–995.

News article announcing to the scientific community that Craig Venter, sponsored by private business interests, plans to sequence the human genome before the Human Genome Project. The piece includes the reactions of other scientists and the difficulties that Venter must overcome.

Pollack, Andrew. "A New Kind of Genomics." *New York Times,* October 21, 2003.

Gives Venter's Sargasso Sea expedition as an example of metagenomics (environmental genomics), the study of the genomes of organisms in an ecosystem as a unit.

———. "Scientist Quits the Company He Led in Quest for Genome." *New York Times,* January 23, 2002.

News story announces that Craig Venter will leave Celera Genomics; the article says he resigned, but in fact he was fired.

Roberts, Leslie. "Gambling on a Shortcut to Genome Sequencing." *Science* 252 (June 21, 1991): 1,618–1,619.

News article accompanying Venter group's article about discovering brain genes through use of expressed sequence tags discusses the technology's possible application to the Human Genome Project and some other scientists' doubts about it.

———. "Genome Patent Fight Erupts." *Science* 254 (October 11, 1991): 184–186.

Describes the controversy raised by the National Institutes of Health's attempt to patent partial sequences of brain genes that Craig Venter and Mark Adams discovered.

Sanders, Laura. "Genome from a Bottle Turns One Bacterium into Another." *Science News* 177 (June 19, 2010): 5–6.

Describes Venter Institute scientists' transplantation of a complete synthetic genome into bacteria and considers whether this constitutes creation of artificial life.

SerVaas, Cory, and Patrick Perry. "For Dr. Craig Venter, Discovery Can't Wait." *Saturday Evening Post* 272 (July 2000): 39 ff.

Long interview with Venter, made shortly after Celera Genomics finished its rough-draft sequence of the human genome.

Shreeve, James. "The Code Breaker." *Discover,* May 1998, pp. 45–51.

Recounts the first part of Venter's career, including TIGR's sequencing of the genomes of Hemophilus influenzae *and other microorganisms.*

Smith, Hamilton O., et al. "Generating a Synthetic Genome by Whole Genome Assembly: Phi-X174 Bacteriophage from Synthetic Oligonucleotides." *Proceedings of the National Academy of Sciences* 100 (December 23, 2003): 15,440–15,445.
Describes Smith's creation of an artificial virus from groups of nucleotides. The virus was able to infect bacteria, just like the natural one.

Venter, J. Craig, and Mark D. Adams. "Shotgun Sequencing of the Human Genome." *Science* 280 (June 5, 1998): 1,540–1,542.
Venter and Adams explain why they believe that their whole-genome shotgun sequencing technique will be able to sequence the human genome with the help of new automated sequencing machines. They also explain their company's business plan and tell what data they intend to make available.

Venter, J. Craig, et al. "Biologically Active Catecholamines Covalently Bound to Glass Beads." *Proceedings of the National Academy of Sciences* 69 (May 1, 1972): 1,141–1,145.
Venter's first scientific paper, published while he was still an undergraduate at the University of California, San Diego. It shows that adrenalin bound to glass beads can still affect the heart, which indicates that this hormone produces changes in cells by binding to receptor molecules on the cells' surfaces.

———. "Environmental Genome Shotgun Sequencing of the Sargasso Sea." *Science* 304 (April 2, 2004): 66–74.
A team from the Venter Institute describes its sampling of water from the Sargasso Sea, mass genome sequencing of the microbes in the samples, and discovery of numerous new genes and species.

———. "The Sequence of the Human Genome." *Science* 291 (February 16, 2001): 1,304–1,351.
The Venter group's scientific paper on their sequencing of a rough draft of the human genome.

Vesely, Rebecca. "Getting Personal: Advances in Biotechnology and the Promises of Personalized Medicine Help Drive Record Investment in 2009." *Modern Healthcare* 40 (February 1, 2010): 26.
Article describes how research on the human genome has led to new tests that use individual genetic information to determine how patients will respond to drugs.

Wade, Nicholas. "Scientist Reveals Genome Secret: It's His." *New York Times,* April 27, 2002.

Craig Venter reveals that most of the human genome DNA that Celera Genomics sequenced came from him.

———. "Scientist's Plan: Map All DNA Within 3 Years." *New York Times,* May 10, 1998.

The first general announcement of Craig Venter's plan to sequence the human genome more quickly and cheaply than the Human Genome Project.

Wadman, Meredith. "Biology's Bad Boy Is Back." *Fortune* 149 (March 8, 2004): 166 ff.

Reviews Venter's career from its beginnings to his announcement that his scientific team has assembled an artificial virus.

Zimmer, Carl. "Tinker, Tailor: Can Venter Stitch Together a Genome from Scratch?" *Science* 299 (February 14, 2003): 1,006–1,007.

Describes Venter's plans to make an artificial microbe that will produce fuel or help the environment in other ways.

Index